Empowered!

Winning the Game of Healthcare

Jim Skinner

Smart Patient Academy
New Braunfels, TX

Empowered! Winning the Game of Healthcare

Copyright © 2016 Jim Skinner

Published by Smart Patient Academy
New Braunfels, TX

Editing, Cover, and Interior Design by Steven W. Booth,
www.GeniusBookServices.com

ISBN-13: 978-0-9887375-4-9

Disclaimer:

This publication contains the opinion and ideas of its author and is solely intended to provide helpful insight and informative material on the subjects addressed. It is sold, understanding that the authors and publisher are not engaged in rendering medical, financial, or any other personal or professional services in the book. The reader should consult with competent professionals before adopting any of the suggestions in this book or drawing inferences from it. The author and publisher specifically disclaim all responsibility for any liability, risk, or loss, both personal and professional, which may be incurred due to the direct or indirect application of any of the principles or suggestions in the book.

Empowered! Winning the Game of Healthcare is not insurance coverage or evidence of coverage. You must enroll and be accepted for insurance coverage with an insurance carrier. With a discrepancy between the contents of this book and your own insurance Plan Documents, the Plan Documents will determine the Plan of Benefits. As used, the term "Plan Documents" includes, but is not limited to, the Booklet, Schedule of Benefits, and any Booklet Amendments/Riders, including any state-specific variations, as applicable. These documents are distributed by your employer and/or directly from the insurance carrier to you. For further details, refer to your insurance Plan Documents.

*This book is dedicated to all those who can bring
a sense of humor into the world of healthcare.
Lord knows, we need it.*

*I have some good news and some bad news. The good news is I can see
now that the cataract surgery went so well. The bad news is I just discovered I've been brushing my teeth with hydrocortisone cream for the last
three weeks!*

—**Frank Curry**, my father-in-law

CONTENTS

SMART PATIENT
ACADEMY

ABOUT THE BOOK

Healthcare, as we all know, can be a stressful topic, because it falls at the crossroads of our money and our health. Managing money requires one skill set and managing medical care requires another. Money and finance can be linear and logical, while medical care can be very subjective and unpredictable. For precisely this reason, we have split this book into two parts: Part I—Smart Patient and Part II—Smart Money. Knowing how to blend both skill sets is critical, and that is the mission of the Smart Patient Academy.

Part I—The Smart Patient section of the book deals with the actual patient experience. This is what you need to know after you buy the insurance, but hopefully before you have a chronic or acute situation. It is also the same information you need to know if you are one of the 40 million Americans serving as a caregiver.

The Smart Patient insights collected by the Smart Patient Academy come from thousands of hours of user experiences as patients and as caregivers. In addition, we have interviewed nearly 100 "High Performance Patients" (HPPs) and High Performance

Caregivers (HPCGs) on our podcast, *Stories with A Purpose,* to create a collection of actionable information that will enable you to extract the most value possible out of the healthcare system.

These models of High Performance Patients can save you months, if not years, of time spent on the normal patient learning curve. But, more importantly, this knowledge can change the outcome of your experience, and that is no small deal. Here are some of the things you will learn:

- How the new healthcare system is organized and how to navigate in it.
- The key organizing principles upon which you can build an effective healthcare strategy.
- How the most resilient people deal with a crisis.

Part II—Smart Money is where you will learn how to be the smartest consumer of healthcare services and insurance. That means you will:

- Determine which health insurance plan is best for you.
- Understand what kind of a healthcare consumer you are.
- Learn how to pay for all this stuff and how to negotiate.
- Make the system work for you, instead of the other way around.

As you master these skills, you will realize that one of the great milestones you can achieve is what we call:

Peace of Mind

- You are in the right place for your medical care.
- You have made good decisions along the way.
- You have left no stone unturned.
- You have taken responsibility for those things in your control and let go of the rest.
- You have a voice.
- You have found a way to live above your circumstance.

There will probably be a number of solutions that you will find in this book that you will want to investigate further. Go to the Helpful Resources section to get those details, downloads, and to generally dig deeper.

We're here to help.

Stay healthy and have fun.

Jim Skinner
March 2016

FOREWORD

Opportunity-Driven Healthcare and You

Not so long ago I attended a health insurance conference, where the featured speaker told the assembled group of mostly insurance professionals the following: "Stop talking about money and start talking about the impact you have on people's lives. People need to know how to use what they have been given and how it is relevant to them."

These words were music to my ears. Why? Like you, I have grown weary of the insurance industry's tendency to focus on the benefits of products and the elegance of insurance buying transactions, instead of the actual user experience as a patient or caregiver. Insurance talk is about money and there seems to be an underlying assumption that once the insurance is in place, the happy employee/consumer will inherently know how to use the product, navigating through the healthcare system without incident. We also assume the employee/consumer will appreciate what they have, simply because it is being sold that way. Reality tells us this is not necessarily so.

I think most would agree there is a huge disconnect between health insurance products and the actual patient experience. I'd like to propose a change. Let's regard the health insurance plans we refer to in this book as *Opportunity-Driven Healthcare*. Why? The word "Opportunity" is more descriptive of the insurance products and the healthcare before you. Opportunity is unrealized potential, which requires our participation to unlock.

Today's opportunity comes in the form of an invitation to engage in your own health. You see, *you* are in charge of your health, not your doctor, not your employer. You. In taking on this role you will not only get the care you need from the healthcare system but you will be a key driver reshaping the healthcare system of the future. The healthcare system and the employer through which health insurance flows need your input and feedback to improve. In essence, they are saying: 'Take the initiative and tell us how to help you. We can all improve the system if we work together. But without your input we can only fix our side (the supply side) of the healthcare equation."

That opportunity is now in front of you. The question is: What will you do with it?

INSIGHT

Health insurance is not health. Health insurance is not a product you consume. Health insurance is a set of tools you use in a process of building and creating an outcome that best fits you.

Here are some of the key messages embedded in this book that all employers want you to know and embrace:

- **Please appreciate the benefits we offer—they cost us an arm and a leg! We are doing the best we can.**
- **Understand we are all in the same "claims boat" together. That means your health affects your co-workers.**
- **Take control of your finances and your health by taking personal responsibility.**
- **We created Wellness programs because we care about you! Participate.**
- **We offer voluntary insurance products because they can help you with the unexpected "shock" expenses we all experience sooner or later.**

PART I
The Smart Patient

CHAPTER 1

Learning How to Fall—Becoming Resilient

> Everyone has a plan until they get hit in the mouth.
> —Mike Tyson, Heavyweight Boxing Champion

I grew up in California on the beachfront and began surfing when I was 5 years old. Like most adventure sports, what begins as fun progressively moves into ever-increasing efforts to push the boundaries of common sense. By the time I was 12 years old, I was spending eight hours in the water daily, searching for the biggest adrenaline rushes possible.

One key feature of getting good at surfing is the ability to relax underwater after a serious wipe-out. I had to learn to stay calm, almost floppy, after falling on the face of a wave two times my height. Over and over, my body would get sucked up in the face of the wave and hurled into space, like a rag-doll, toward a menacing reef just below the surface. This is called going "over the falls." But it doesn't end there. After that, I'd get held underwater, tumbled, and pummeled by the overwhelming power of the wave.

I figured out that coping with the turbulence meant I had to to-tally relax, let my body go limp, and skid on the water, not dive. That way, I would not penetrate the water deeply and hit the reef just below. I had to let go and stop fighting a force I could not control. Oddly enough, relaxing allowed me to stay underwater twice as long, because I didn't burn up all my energy on the fight. I learned how to fall. And without knowing it, I learned the first key to resilience in any situation—relax.

With practice, we labeled this insanity as "fun" and intentionally would seek ever-bigger "body-wamping" surf that would chal-lenge even the most adventurous person's ability to relax. For me, it was all play. But the deeper and more lasting lesson it taught me was how reframing an event can transform naturally terrifying into something positive. And this is the second key to resilience: event reframing. I like to call this emotional Ju Jit Su.

INSIGHT

We seek adversity and call it adventure. Adversity seeks us, and we call it a problem. In the end, they are both opportunities to grow.

When I was diagnosed with stage three colon cancer at age 42, I was in uncharted waters, facing the most challenging waves of confusion, fear, and chaos of my life. I clearly was not ready to be pounded by the disease and was surprised by the numerous obstacles imposed by the healthcare system.

To my surprise, the entire experience was not the linear, pre-dictable process I had been sold or anticipated. My strategy was simple: Be compliant. I figured I would follow the rules, and the healthcare system would take care of me. Boy, was I wrong.

The experience was very complex, full of subjective judgments and contradictions, error prone, and took longer than I imagined possible. The situation required my most creative problem-solving skills and demanded tremendous emotional flexibility and resilience I did not know I had.

With the help of family, we built a support team to coordinate the advice and communication from five doctors who were all doing their own thing. No one told us to do this. There were no models to follow. We just used common sense. The entire experience was improvised.

One thing I never anticipated was how alone you can feel while going through a major medical crisis. There is a Mount Everest-sized learning curve to climb. It was as if nobody had colon cancer before me. There was no experience from which I could draw. Much to my surprise, nobody takes responsibility to help you navigate through the maze, either. It is not the doctor's job, nor the hospital's job, nor the pharmacist's, nor the insurance company's role.

Whose job is it to help you navigate the complexities of the system? How do you balance going to "war" with a disease and the inevitable collateral damage that war inflicts on you, emotionally and spiritually? To a large degree, you and your family are on your own. This situation leaves you with three balls to juggle: the disease, the emotional battles, and a medical system, designed around itself, not the patient.

The irony is that I am an expert in the health insurance field. I have family and friends who are doctors, and I received help from all of them. Despite their help, I still got pummeled and disoriented, and felt defeated. At least, that is where I began, but it is not where I ended.

Just four short years after the colon cancer, when I was diagnosed with an unrelated brain tumor, I was much better prepared. Oddly enough, the cancer experience had trained me to become a confident, "high performance" patient. This time, I managed the quantity of care that fit me and skillfully surfed through waves of conflicting opinions. I even successfully negotiated several medical bills with providers. I was empowered and got second opinions from over twenty-two doctors, which was necessary, because they contradicted each other so frequently!

I worked the system. The system did not work me, because I had learned skills that made me effective. I could rise above my circumstance, relax in the emotional turbulence, and see opportunity, normally hidden by fear, anxiety, and the way I had been programmed to think about healthcare.

I'm here to tell you:

- You *can* take control of your healthcare situation.
- You *can* make the healthcare system work for you, not against you.
- You *can* conquer confusion, fear, and intimidation. And you don't have to wait for a healthcare crisis.
- What you'll learn in this book will change the quality of your life—in sickness or in health.

Notes & Ideas

CHAPTER 2

A Whole New World—How Did We Get Here?

For better or worse, many of the effects of Healthcare Reform— aka Obamacare—are here to stay, independent of what happens politically. It is important to understand that the healthcare system is undergoing the most radical change since the introduction of Medicare in 1964. There is a new healthcare environment out there, and it requires a new healthcare consumer—that's YOU! The Smart Patient.

With all the debate around healthcare it is rare that anyone discusses what is driving the need for change. The answer is demographics. There are about 78 million Baby Boomers who are retiring. As they do, they will move from commercial, employer-paid insurance to the Medicare market at about 10,000 people per day. Why is this a problem? Because Medicare prices are government controlled and artificially low. These low government-driven Medicare prices are subsidized by the under-65 health insurance market. In short, younger workers are there to support older retirees.

Unfortunately, there are way too many people moving into Medicare for this model to be sustainable. The Medicare model, created in 1964, when people only lived on average to age 68, is built on a faulty assumption: that people would only live 3-5 years on Medicare. Some economists estimate that the funding gap between what has been promised to future Medicare beneficiaries and what we have money to pay for is close to $100 trillion! *That is trillion with a "T".*

Clearly something has to change. There are two basic philosophical approaches to managing this problem: the government as a solution or the customer as a solution. For the past five years the healthcare policy pendulum has been aggressively pushed toward the government as the solution. Health reform has essentially been a reorganization of healthcare "supply"—hospitals, doctors, and insurance companies.

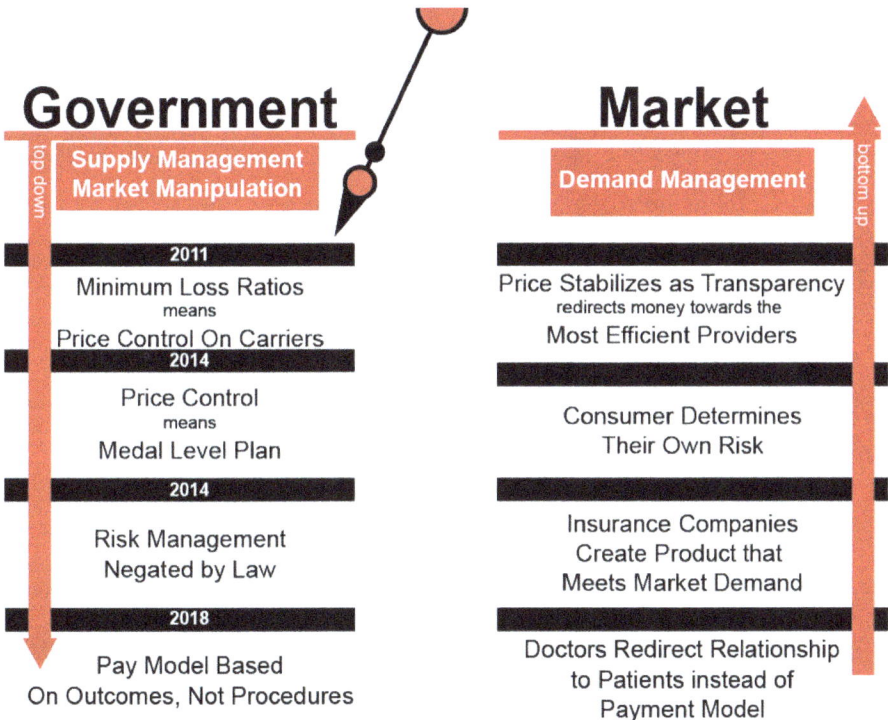

Government

top down

**Supply Management
Market Manipulation**

2011
Minimum Loss Ratios
means
Price Control On Carriers

2014
Price Control
means
Medal Level Plan

2014
Risk Management
Negated by Law

2018
Pay Model Based
On Outcomes, Not Procedures

Market

bottom up

Demand Management

Price Stabilizes as Transparency
redirects money towards the
Most Efficient Providers

Consumer Determines
Their Own Risk

Insurance Companies
Create Product that
Meets Market Demand

Doctors Redirect Relationship
to Patients instead of
Payment Model

Practically speaking, how does the health reform affect me? Most people would point to the fact that today everybody must have health insurance or pay a fine. But the fine is simply a very small symptom of a massive change. The more permanent change is the role we play as patients and caregivers. We now have a whole new level of responsibility that is being given to us but it is likely that nobody is telling you this. We need to recognize and assume our new roles in order to extract the value we want out of the healthcare system we use.

One of the main sources of confusion is how we have been trained to think about healthcare. It is generally assumed that we can consume our way to health with more prescriptions, more surgeries, higher technology, more insurance, more supplements, and more exercise equipment. Somebody creates. We consume. The mentality is: "Just fix me, doc!" But taking this passive, consumption-oriented approach is not just ineffective; it could be lethal!

INSIGHT

Let's be clear. *Taking initiative and control is work!* Staying healthy and getting the outcomes you need is a creative process that requires your best problem solving skills, not your consuming skills. Simply sitting back on a healthcare conveyor belt that dishes out cookie cutter care is a sure recipe for frustration and bad outcomes.

Old System	New System
The insurance industry and the healthcare system trained you to be like this	The new healthcare marketplace DEMANDS you become this!
Passive	Active
Dependent	Independent
Unaware	Hyper-Aware
Unconfident	Assertive
Isolated	Collaborative
Unintentional	Focused
Not Responsible	Personally Responsible
Unresourceful	Resourceful
Paralyzed	Innovative
Focused on Past	Focused on Future

WHICH HEALTHCARE SYSTEM ARE YOU IN?

Let's call the old system the HMO world—you know, that passive world, where you have been taught to think the doctor's job is to fix you. In this scenario, you simply show up, shut-up, take the medicine, and be compliant. Here is the problem with that. Compliance disables most of us by substituting our own initiative and creativity with an external solution or quick fix, mostly designed to manage symptoms. Most of us accept a symptom management approach because it is fast, easy, and relatively predictable. But passive patients end up frustrated and generally sicker over time. In this old "Happy-Meals" healthcare system, what motivation do we have to work toward our own health when we can be spoon fed a quick temporary fix? We think that is as good as it gets. Not so.

It is important to understand that healthcare is in a transition period right now. It is pretty clear that yesterday's model that encouraged the passive consumption of medical care is not working to improve our health or lower costs. How do we know this? In a nutshell we are spending more and getting less. Some 70% of 2+ trillion dollars of our healthcare spending is driven by "lifestyle"-based diseases. And the lifetime cost of care is now estimated to be about $316,000 and is going up. The stats go on and on, but I think most of us already know that things are not working well.

Change has to occur. And here is the key: that change is staring at you in the mirror. You and I are the now the agents of change. We need to assume this role mostly for our own good, and as we do so we improve the industry as a whole. I know you did not vote for this new role and perhaps you don't even want this new role, but it is the reality of our time.

More importantly, we have an opportunity on our hands, not a problem. It is pretty apparent what does not work, but we don't fully understand what does work. And while most of us can understand we have new responsibility, we simply don't know what that means. We don't know when to be passive, when to be assertive, or how to navigate any of the complexities and obstacles that confront us.

Let's start by defining what does work. Doctors use the word "compliance," but they really want your "engagement." They need you as a partner in your healthcare, not as a consumer of products and services. Here is what that looks like.

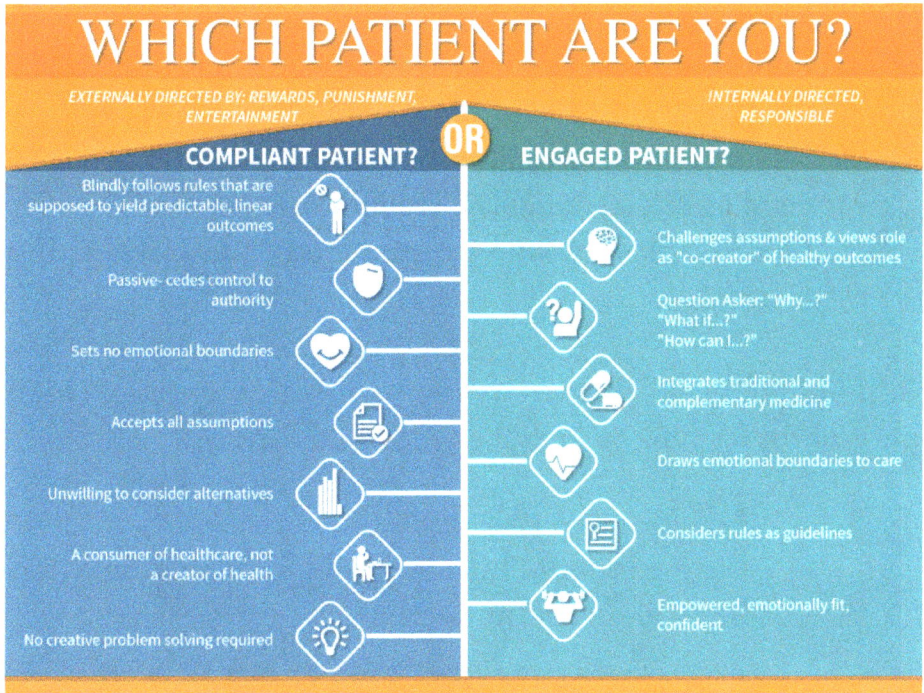

WHICH PATIENT ARE YOU?

EXTERNALLY DIRECTED BY: REWARDS, PUNISHMENT, ENTERTAINMENT

INTERNALLY DIRECTED, RESPONSIBLE

COMPLIANT PATIENT?   OR   ENGAGED PATIENT?

Blindly follows rules that are supposed to yield predictable, linear outcomes

Passive- cedes control to authority

Sets no emotional boundaries

Accepts all assumptions

Unwilling to consider alternatives

A consumer of healthcare, not a creator of health

No creative problem solving required

Challenges assumptions & views role as "co-creator" of healthy outcomes

Question Asker: "Why...?" "What if...?" "How can I...?"

Integrates traditional and complementary medicine

Draws emotional boundaries to care

Considers rules as guidelines

Empowered, emotionally fit, confident

Some Good News!

While many aspects of the top–down government approach are not working, there is one promising trend that is beginning to put the customers/patients/caregivers back in the driver's seat. Payments to doctors will increasingly move toward healthy outcomes in the future. That means providers get paid for keeping you healthy and they get rewarded for a great patient experience. This new payment model will begin to replace a system where providers were paid on the quantity of procedures they performed. This new payment model alone is revolutionary. Why? Rebuilding healthcare around the customer is the single best way to spur innovation of quality and lower costs because customer-centered care will respond to our feedback.

Today a whole new generation of doctors is being trained in medical schools in the art of "Shared Decision Making. SDM, as it is called in medical circles, is a complicated way of saying "let's listen to the patient for a change." Wow! Can you imagine somebody actually listening to your healthcare story and your insights into your own health? As dumb as this sounds, SDM is a revolutionary way of delivering traditional medical care in this country. But, as good as this sounds, SDM is built on an assumption that you and I know the new role we are supposed to play, and that we play that role.

In short, the new healthcare system is about *Engagement*. This is great news! It's time to grab the wheel and drive.

> "...I assumed that my hospital and every hospital in the world would do everything they could to get the latest information and bring it to the table. That is a common and wrong assumption. Don't expect medicine to know everything and do everything. Get involved and do what you can too."
>
> "...once upon a time humanity thought the earth was the center of the solar system, but as we got better telescopes and made better observations it turns out that the behavior of the planets didn't work like that. Eventually astronomers had to dump their old way of thinking and say, "Oh, the earth isn't the center of the solar system." Something similar is happening regarding patients. Historically, patients have kind of orbited around the doctors. But now the modern approach is patient centered care..."
>
> **Dave Debronkart** ("E-Patient Dave")—*survivor of Stage 4 Kidney Cancer*—Patient Activist; Author—"Let Patient Help", A Patient Engagement Handbook—excerpt from *Stories With A Purpose*

Notes & Ideas

CHAPTER 3

The New Field of Play

Where do we start our training? What is the critical first step in becoming a "High Performance Patient" (HPP) or "High Performance Caregiver" (HPCG)? We begin with "**situational awareness.**" Simply put, situational awareness (SA) means:

- Knowing where you are, physically and emotionally.
- Seeing what is going on around you.
- Understanding how it all impacts you.

Whenever we take up anything new, like a job, a sport, or a hobby, at least somebody explains to us the rules of the game. That is not to say there is no learning curve. I am simply saying that we have some basic knowledge about how many strokes it takes to shoot a "par" in golf, or where the fifty yard line is in football. In short we know what the field of play looks like. But somehow, in healthcare, the field of play is not so clearly understood and sometimes winning can't always be a proverbial cure.

Here is a picture of what the new field of healthcare looks like. This knowledge alone will impact how you play the game.

Level 1 Situational Awareness

Overall Trends You Need to Know

- Doctor-Patient relationships become a collaboration to co-create outcomes. More responsibility shifts to patient.
- A big drive toward "data driven medicine" is here. A conflict between production-line medicine and personalized medicine is developing. Wearable technology is a big part of the data game.
- Providers will increasingly be paid for healthy outcomes, instead of the number of procedures they perform. A good "patient experience" becomes a financial driver.
- Massive hospital consolidation, coordination of medical records, and care integration is evolving. These organizations will have many names but they are essentially teams dedicated to your care.
- Telemedicine and virtual visits are becoming more common.
- Due to high error rates, hospital safety scores become important and more transparent.
- Patients begin to have access and input into their own medical records.
- Complimentary medicine—Chinese, Ayurveda, and Botanical—will be blended with traditional

medicine. Why? In many cases they can be more effective and cost less.

- Doctors have about 12 minutes to see you and 78,000 procedure codes to sort through. Realistically, you have 6 minutes of their attention. Use it wisely.
- State of the art healthcare is evolving so rapidly that second opinion services become more common to keep up.
- Nutrition as medicine is more readily accepted by traditional doctors.
- Science validates "mind-body" medicine and drives a "mindfulness" movement. Psycho Neural Immunology (PNI) is this new field of science. How you think impacts gene expression. It all means that "you are what you think."
- Price shopping medical services is huge as massive price disparities are revealed to the general public.

Most of us over-estimate what the healthcare system can do for us and under-estimate what we can do for ourselves. The reality is that very small changes targeted to the right areas of our lives can have a very large positive impact when done consistently over long periods of time.

Maybe you have heard of the "magic of compound interest" in building your financial wealth? Well, apply this same principle to your physical, mental, and emotional health. The same compounding impact will occur when we simply commit to improving our health. The point is we do not necessarily need to make radical or big changes, nor is it necessary to do it all at once. Ease into change at your own pace. Be consistent. Improve.

Level 2 Situational Awareness

At several points in this book, references are made to that fact that being a passive consumer of healthcare is dangerous. This list of danger zones is not an exaggeration to make a point. Unfortunately, these are shocking realities that are mostly not discussed in the field of healthcare. Knowing where the potholes are in the road ahead can help you avoid a major accident. Healthcare is no different. Read this and you'll see what I mean.

Danger Zones, Potholes, and Blind Curves

- Medical errors are the third leading cause of death in the United States! That adds up to nearly 440,000 deaths per year. A high percentage of these errors happen in hospitals. There is no need to be a victim. Learn the hospital safety scores in your area.

- The Mayo Clinic conservatively estimates that nearly 25% of patients receive an incorrect diagnosis. Over 50% receive the wrong treatment plan. Get at least one second opinion and preferably diversify those second opinions with doctors that bridge the gap between holistic and traditional medicine. These docs are called Complementary or Functional physicians.

- It takes an average 17 years for a new standard of care to be adopted by 50% of physicians in the United States. This is known as the "lethal time lag." Don't be afraid or intimidated to question assumptions, standards, and protocols.

Your care may just fall into this lethal lag time category.

- Curing disease is about the physical. Healing is about the emotional and spiritual. You can frequently have one without the other. Traditional medical care is restricted to the physical. To heal, you are on you own.

- If you have a chronic illness, you are largely in a symptom management system that may never address the origin of the disease. Trust what your body is telling you and find a provider who digs into the origins of the disease.

- Direct to consumer advertising by the pharmaceutical industry is driving you toward the most profitable drug, not necessarily the most effective. Higher technology, more medicine, and more data can sometimes cause more harm than good. Low tech, non-invasive procedures and techniques are good. Be careful what you ask for.

The Organizing Principle Upon Which to Build a Healthcare Strategy

Now that we have gotten some insight into the healthcare field of play, it is pretty clear that you need to be on your toes when navigating your way through the healthcare system. One of the key organizing principles upon which you can build any healthcare strategy is creative problem solving or "thinking outside the box."

Let's call "the box" a narrow range of possibilities or a set of limiting beliefs. We all have them and doctors are no different. This does not make them bad doctors. It just makes them human. Good doctors recognize these limitations and form teams to counterbalance their confirmation biases. Good doctors listen to you and are not threatened by your engagement. But they are not all this way. You need to be aware which type of doctor you are dealing with.

Thinking outside the box requires you to recognize that you are in a box to begin with. Compliance is simply a strict adherence to the box of standards, rules, and protocols that have been created by others. Sometimes these standards work well and sometimes they cause more damage.

The trick is that compliance-driven doctors do not recognize or acknowledge that they are in a box of limited possibilities constrained by:

- Only what can be measured and quantified.
- The scope of what was taught in medical school, sometimes many years ago.
- How current they are on new ways to handle old problems.

But don't be discouraged or surprised when a compliance-driven doctor smugly says "Who went to medical school here?" This reaction to your engagement is generally coming from a doctor who is more hung up on being correct than helping you think through a solution to your care. You definitely did not go to medical school! But that is what makes you the perfect person to think outside the box. You can gently redirect and debate your doctor. That is to be expected. But don't always think you need to agree.

Your job is to have one foot in the box and one foot outside the box. This strategy will give you the balance you need to see creative alternatives that social scientists call "the adjacent possible." Some solutions are right next to us but we never see them because we stay in the confines of the box. Thinking outside the box can save your life.

Here is an example. Dave DeBronkart, aka E-Patient Dave as he is known in the world of patient advocacy, is a great example of how thinking outside the box can save your life. Diagnosed with Stage 4 kidney cancer and given only six months to live, Dave threw caution to the wind and did a deep dive into the online patient community world. Dave learned quickly from other patients like him about a life-saving approach to his disease which had been overlooked previously. In short, Dave brought the life-saving solution to his providers. That was nearly five years ago. Today Dave is cancer free and now teaches what he learned to medical schools all over the country.

In short, High Performance Patients (HPPs) and High Performance Caregivers (HPCGs) are engaged in the process and they are not afraid to color outside the lines. This is how they win, and you can too. Sometimes your doctor will take you beautifully over the finish line. Sometimes you need to carry your doctor with you to the finish line. Either way, you need to win. Don't be intimidated. The process of healthcare is a collaboration, not a parent–child relationship.

Notes & Ideas

CHAPTER 4

Five Keys You Need to Know

The Smart Patient Academy produces a podcast, called **Stories With A Purpose (SWAP)**, in which we ask people who have gone through the most harrowing medical crises you can imagine the following question: "What do you know now that you wished you knew when you were first diagnosed?" The answers to this question have enabled us to develop models and patterns of behavior which can be copied. In fact, the SWAP show is where we developed the concept of "high performance patients" because these patients are more than just "survivors." They have gone on to thrive.

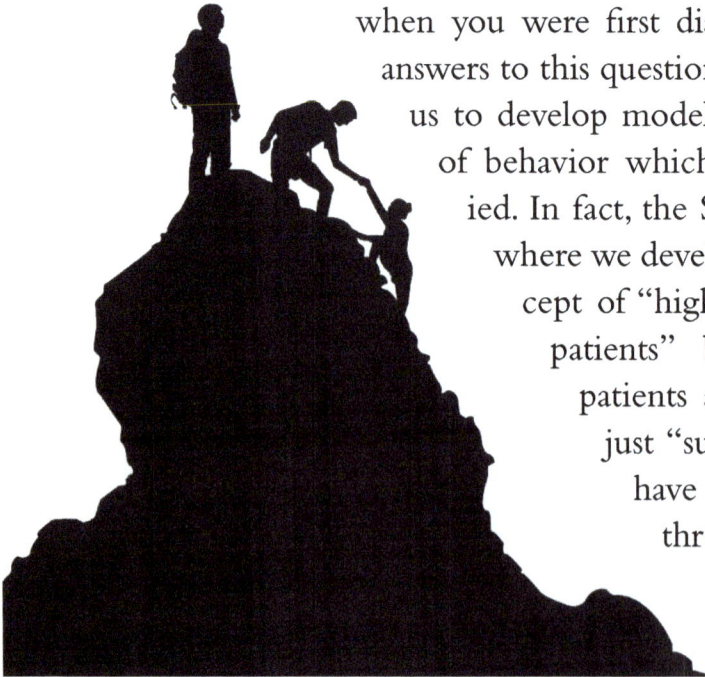

Here are five critical characteristics about the healthcare system, distilled from these interviews. You will notice that we have presented these insights as obstacles first and as opportunities second.

Obstacle #1: Health insurance only covers about 50% of all effective healing solutions available. As patients, we limit our scope of what we see as a healing strategy to only those things "covered by insurance." That leaves a whole world of healing solutions that most of us never consider. We have an additional problem with doctors who regard their medical training as the sum total of all healing solutions available. Believe it or not, most medical schools do not study the science of nutrition, making nutrition-based treatment strategies outside the scope of their care. The limits we impose on ourselves and the limits set up by doctors sets up a perfect storm that serves neither of us well.

Opportunity #1: There are tons of alternative treatments that can be less expensive and more effective than traditional techniques with almost no side effects! Healthcare that integrates functional medicine with traditional care is becoming a trend but, in the meantime, we need to expand our definition of healing options. Do not wait for the healthcare industry to do this for you. You need help now. Seek "Integrative Medicine" or "Functional Medicine" doctors to bridge the two worlds. They are more inclined to address the origin of disease instead of simply managing symptoms. These docs will push more responsibility and work on to you, but their approach to medicine is a collaboration not a compliance game.

Obstacle #2: Ironically, the same system that leads the world in cutting edge drugs and high-tech surgical procedures, saving countless lives, is the same system that is the third leading cause of death in the United States! You read that correctly. Medical

Spectrum of Healing Strategies

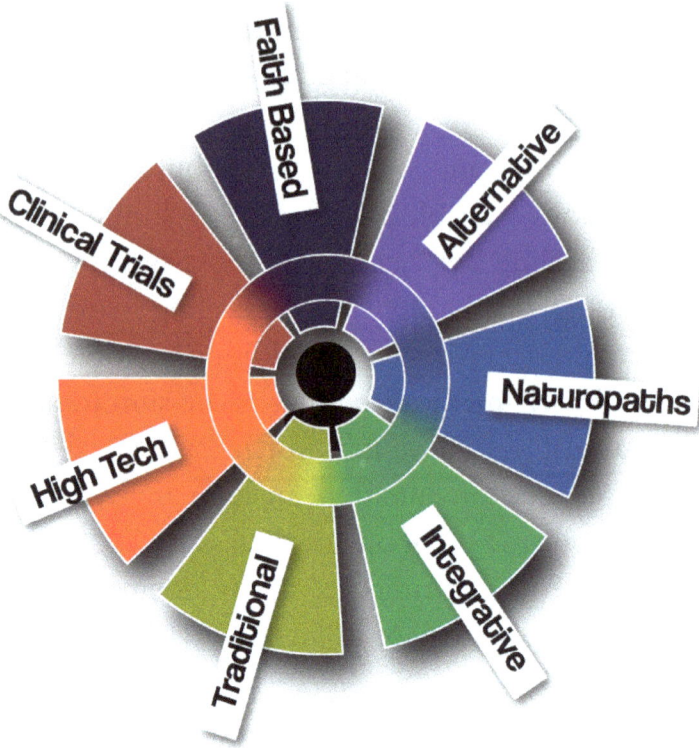

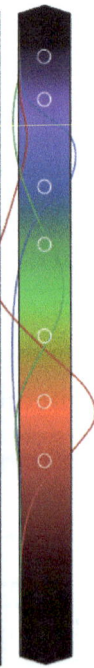

- Faith Based
- Alternative Medicine
- Naturopaths & Complimentary
- Integrative
- Traditional
- High Tech
- Clinical Trials

errors are the third leading cause of death. The point is not to scare you. The point is to inform you there are big potholes on the healthcare superhighway, and you need to be careful. Don't assume everyone knows what they are doing.

Most of us look in the wrong places for these errors. Patient safety experts tell us that it is generally the cumulative effect of many little mistakes and lapses of judgement that trigger a calamity. And these errors tend to happen in the arena of low-tech human miscommunication, most frequently during shift changes in a hospital in what is referred to as a pass-off methodology. It is not most of the time any single, one-off, massive error.

"The shocking truth is that some large, prestigious hospitals have four to five times the complication rates of other hospitals in the same city. And within good hospitals, pockets of poorly performing services abound.

Medicine is its own culture. It has its own language, ethos, and code of justice. How a doctor approaches a patient's problem and whether he or she takes care of it...depends to a large extent on the institution's workplace culture. At some medical centers, profits are king, while at others teamwork is a core value."

—Marty Makary MD, MPH, Author of *Unaccountable*, surgeon and associate professor at Johns Hopkins School of Public Health.

Opportunity #2: Step 1: Make sure you are in the right place! That means you have the checked out the hospital safety scores and feel confident that you have picked the most safety conscious facility available.

Step 2: Form a team and designate a "wingman" or "patient navigator" to help you make great decisions, communicate with providers, and monitor nursing shift changes as best you can. Most times your wingman will be family. But supplement your team with others like the nursing staff, your insurance broker, employee assistance program people, pharmacists, or even Human Resources folks at your company. Sometimes, the best teams are combinations of all these people. If you want to hire a professional, know that there are professional navigators and advocates whose services you can buy.

Step 3: See what opportunity, tools, or resources are in front of you already. Use our *Constellation of Opportunity* (Chapter 8) to identify who to recruit to your high performance caregiving team. These are your allies. Use them.

Obstacle #3: *Best Doctors* is the leading second opinion medical organization in the world. The *Best Doctors* program was born out of Harvard's Medical School. They have worked with tens of thousands of patients since the 1980s and, get this, they change or modify medical diagnoses 33% of the time and recommend treatment changes in 75% of all cases they review! That is an astoundingly high disparity rate, which reminds us that healthcare is full of grey areas, best guesses, and judgment calls. Be it a subjective judgment or a clear error, it does not matter. Either way, we have to live with the consequences.

Opportunity #3: Get a second and even a third opinion. Realize the explosion of quality medical information and the existence of expert patient navigators makes it possible for the patient to know more than their doctor about the latest trends in care for your specific condition. Hard to believe, but true. Also dig into the online patient community and learn quickly from others like you. None of this makes you a doctor! It makes you an informed patient, thinking outside the box, confident enough to ask questions. It is astounding how often you can improve the outcome of your care by asking these simple questions.

- Why are we doing this…?
- What if…there were a natural, non-invasive approach?
- How can I…?
- What would you do if this was your mother?

Obstacle #4: Traditional medical science has the tools to validate what "alternative" providers have said all along. Negative emotion working through our hormones and our immune systems gets trapped in our bodies and can be toxic over long periods of time. This emotional toxicity is metabolized in our bodies as inflammation, which can create a disease state—think autoimmune problems, whose source we can't easily detect.

> The tendency to ignore our emotions is old think, a remnant of the still-reigning paradigm that keeps us focused on the material level of health, the physicality of it.
>
> —**Candace B. Pert,** Ph.D., author of *Molecules of Emotion*

As previously described, the emerging field of science that links our emotional health with our physical health is called Psycho Neural Immunology (PNI). But here is one of the really cool things about PNI. The negative emotion that causes silent in-flammation works equally well in a positive direction. Powerful, deeply felt spiritual emotions can create a positive anti-inflam-matory response as well. In short, the reaction we have to our environment has a dramatic impact on our health. The old adage, "You are what you eat," is true. But it is equally true to say: "You are what you think."

> The critical element is the awareness that you've got to be involved in your own healing. How you come to the event is at least is important as whatever malady it is that you've got. You have some choice. We de-emphasized people's personal participation in the process, but most illness, especially chronic illness doesn't lend itself to either an easy fix or technological repair that gives us an immediacy of return.
>
> How you come to your disease is critically important. If you don't come to it with an open heart and a sense of awakened soul, knowing that you have some choice, then you dramatically underutilize your power to heal. That is the bottom line. People need to somehow find ways to kindle that soulful light within that gives them hope and allows them to participate in their own healing, because that is going to make the critical difference.
>
> —**Dr. Carl Hammerschlaug**, Pioneer of Psycho Neural Immunology, author of numerous books, Partner to Dr. Patch Adams, and renowned psychiatrist. Excerpt from *Stories With A Purpose*

PSYCHO NEURAL IMMUNOLOGY FOR DUMMIES

You Are What You Think

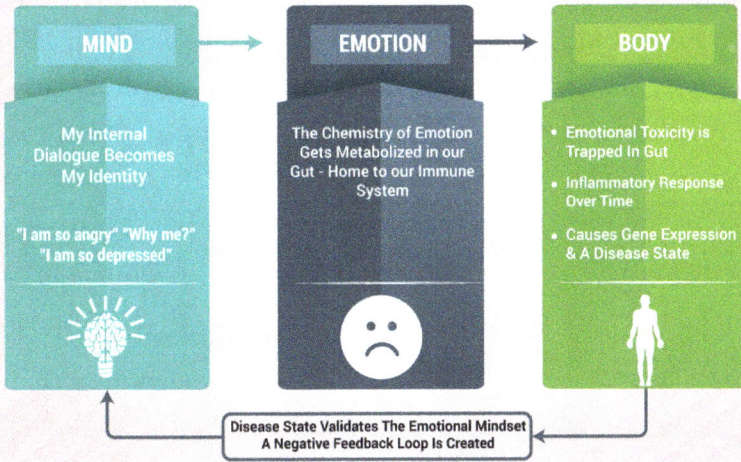

MIND → **EMOTION** → **BODY**

MIND
My Internal Dialogue Becomes My Identity

"I am so angry". "Why me?" "I am so depressed"

EMOTION
The Chemistry of Emotion Gets Metabolized in our Gut - Home to our Immune System

BODY
• Emotional Toxicity is Trapped In Gut

• Inflammatory Response Over Time

• Causes Gene Expression & A Disease State

Disease State Validates The Emotional Mindset
A Negative Feedback Loop Is Created

Opportunity #4: In our study of High Performance Patients, we have discovered specific emotional pathways and triggers used by these resilient people and their caregivers. Their ability is not random and can be learned. There are certain things they do that enable them to tap into a deep natural reservoir of emotional and spiritual virtues that resonate deep within their core identity. This process is natural, and the catalyst or trigger is deep, proactive gratitude—the granddaddy of all spiritual emotions.

Because gratitude is so counter-intuitive in the midst of adversity, we have created an application called *The Opportunity Coach.* This application will enable you to discharge negative emotion and to reintroduce and infuse your psyche with the most positive, emotional anti-inflammatory available: deeply felt thankfulness or gratitude. The daily practice of infusing your psyche with deep gratitude has been proven to increase dopamine levels, doing much the same as an anti-depressant. A thankful mindset can, over time, improve our physical health, as well as our overall effectiveness and enjoyment of life. Consider *The Opportunity Coach* as an emotional nutrition program enabling you to become ever-more emotionally fit and flexible.

But here is the big bonus! *The Opportunity Coach* will also make you a better decision maker. Why? Fear and anxiety are pretty normal reactions to a medical situation and these emotions cloud our judgment. *The Opportunity Coach* and the gratitude principles upon which it is founded will give you a process for stepping outside the emotional storms long enough to gain a new perspective. The ability to make good decisions requires perspective, especially in the midst of adversity.

> "To be honest I would say that the experience of being ill itself taught me a tremendous amount of resilience...how can I break free from suffering and develop a kind of resilience to liberate myself into the moment to deal with what actually is happening, rather than how I think it should be."
>
> "...if you experience and express gratitude for the circumstances of your life, you tend to be much happier. Your immune system is stronger. Your heart functions get better. Your blood pressure can go down. People who commit to the practices of grateful living change their lives immeasurably."
>
> —**Kristi Nelson,** *survivor of Stage 4 Lymphoma while in her thirties,* Executive Director, A Network for Grateful Living (www.gratefulness.org)—excerpt from *Stories With A Purpose*

Obstacle #5: Most of us love our doctors. I love mine too. That said, there are good doctors operating as best they can in a bad system. And that may be the crux of the problem we face in getting the care we need—the proverbial "system." How many times have you heard some customer service rep tell you: "The system doesn't allow me to…" Just fill in the blank. My question has always been, who manages the system—a human or another system?" To the customer it feels as if a bunch of bureaucratic drones checked common sense at the door of their workplace and replaced it with protocols, shortcuts, and habits that serve the system, not the customer. This phenomenon happens in every facet of society and workplace culture. Healthcare is not different. Unfortunately, nobody is accountable when a system is in charge.

This is why it is important to be engaged first, compliant second in a healthcare setting. Excessive deference to authority, protocols and compliance regimes can be dangerous to your health. What if the assumptions that underlie the standard of care you are following are just flat out wrong? It happens all the time.

Consider these examples.

Example 1: Shortly after X-ray machines became a standard of care in the 1950s, doctors routinely X-rayed pregnant women. After thousands of babies were born with cancer and other maladies, the standard of care was finally changed. Do you know how long it took to correct this lethal issue? Answer: 20 years!

Example 2: For over two decades nutrition standards emphasized low fat, low protein, high carb diets. Avoid red meat. Eat no eggs. Use margarine instead of butter. Most of us went out of our way to follow the protocols of the day. Today the standard is almost the reverse: Eat high fat foods (the good ones). Keep carb intake low.

Eggs are the perfect food. Sugar is the newest villain in the war on silent inflammation. Do you know how long it took to start moving in the right direction? Answer: 20 years.

Example 3: Prescriptions for opioid-based painkillers has increased 400% since the year 2000. Drug overdose deaths are up 140%. Some 61% of drug overdose deaths are linked to the prescription opioid painkillers Oxycodone and Fentanyl. Why? Symptom management healthcare has been driving unchecked drug dispensing. Numerous compliant patients with back pain, neck pain, sciatica, and rheumatoid arthritis have gotten hooked on these opioid drugs with very little consequence to the dispensing entities. None of these statistics take into account the massive increase in heroin use and deaths linked directly to addiction whose origin has been legal prescription medication liberally dispensed through the healthcare system. It has only been very recently that the first steps have been taken to address this problem. What has been the lethal time-lag in this instance? Answer: 16 years.

Opportunity #5: You need to think outside the compliance box. That means you question assumptions and trust what your body is telling you when you have doubts. Ask questions. Engage. There are no dumb questions. It is also very smart to get multiple opinions from a variety of sources. It will give you the peace of mind you need to know you are on the right track in the first place.

Notes & Ideas

CHAPTER 5

Healthcare Built for Human Behavior

For those of us who are managing a chronic or acute illness, or as a caregiver of someone like that, understand the structural flaw in healthcare that fragments physical care from emotional care. The world of hyper-specialization breaks us into body parts as if there were no overlap between them. As a patient, we are left to integrate these worlds ourselves.

The metaphors we use to physically "attack," "combat," or "go to war" with disease are precisely the opposite metaphors we need to stay emotionally and spiritually healthy. The more we attack, physically, the more damage we do, emotionally. The problem is you and I, as patients, are left to pick up the collateral damage caused by the physical side. The doctors causing the damage, frequently, will not even acknowledge the role their approach takes on the emotional side. This is what patients are referring to when they complain about healthcare being "demeaning."

Healthcare built for human behavior is built around the totality of the patient experience. Healthcare built for human behavior integrates the science of curing disease with the art of healing. Think of it this way: the doctor works from the outside-in, and the patient works from the inside-out. Both parties work together to co-create the optimal outcome which blends a physical cure with emotional and spiritual healing. The two meet somewhere in the middle.

We have identified three battlefronts. Let's call the physical battlefront, "The Way of War," the emotional battlefront, "The Way of Opportunity," and the spiritual battlefront is, "The Way of Peace." Balancing all three looks like this:

Healthcare Built for Human Behavior

The Way of Opportunity
Emotional
- Awareness
- Creative
- Subjective
- Internal
- Right Brain
- Self Reliant

The Way of War
Physical
- Interventions
- Technology
- Logical
- External
- Left Brain
- Compliance Driven

The Way of Peace
Spiritual
- Heart
- Intuition
- Transformative
- Dependent
- God Driven

Healthcare Built for Human Behavior should be empathetic, responsive, collaborative, competent, hollistic, multi-disciplinary, transparent, and affordable. It is time we demand what we deserve. This is what an engaged patient and integrative healthcare system can accomplish when they work together.

Notes & Ideas

CHAPTER 6

Engagement—What High Performance Patients Do

> **INSIGHT**
>
> *The world teaches that we should fix a problem first, and then things will feel fine. High Performance Patients and High Performance Caregivers adjust their perspective first so that the problem loses the emotional power that skews good decision-making. HPPs work on fixing the details of the problem after they have achieved some level of mental clarity and emotional calm.*

One of the critical lessons I learned from my cancer experience is that the outcomes of my medical care are co-created by my doctor and me. Co-creation means the two of us work out a solution together. I learned I could not sit back and passively consume care as a "patient" patient. I had several key roles to play that most doctors just assume you know. I had to learn to create value out of a situation where there seemingly was none.

Here is what happened to me.

Not too many years ago, three neurosurgeons, a physicist, and a herd of nurses drilled screws into my head to hold a scaffold in place while they laid out their plan of attack on my brain. There, in front of them, was the most elaborate 8 foot by 10 foot, three dimensional photo of my brain. It appeared like they were planning a lunar landing.

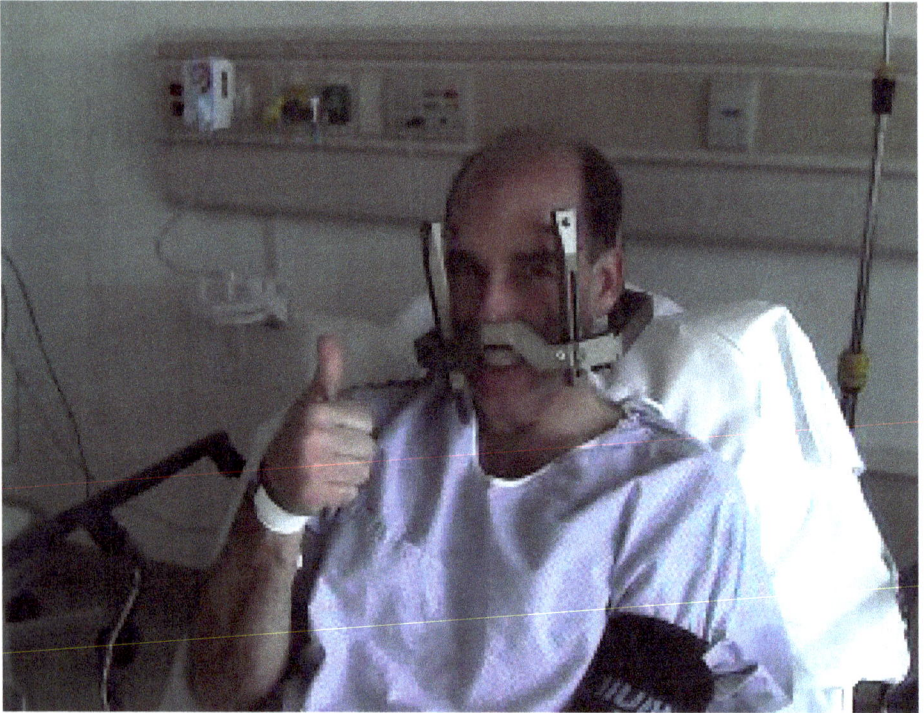

They were about to embark on the surgical procedure called Gamma Knife. The goal was to disable a tumor located very close to my brain stem that was, basically, too dangerous to operate on in the traditional brain surgery way.

As I mentioned before, not everything in healthcare goes according to plan. Uh Oh #1. The surgery disabled the tumor, they think, but in doing so, they also knocked-out my balance and hearing on my left side. The worst side effect of the surgery was the incredible vertigo. My brain would randomly and without warning make me think I was upside down.

Can you imagine calmly sitting in your chair at work and then suddenly you feel like are falling? About a month after the surgery, I flew out of a perfectly good chair, throwing my coffee in the air as I "fell." I ended up on the floor in front of several stunned onlookers. For them, it must have been hilarious to watch, but it was scary stuff for me.

To correct this problem, my neurosurgeon tried what he had been trained to do. He put me on powerful steroids for several months, explaining the steroids would calm the inflammation of my balance nerve. Uh Oh #2. Not only did the steroids not work, they nearly killed me. After four months of this nonsense, with no progress, the surgeon gave up saying: "I have pretty much run out of options for you. Have you ever tried Gingko Biloba? We have no idea why it would work, but some of our patients have reported to us that it does. Maybe it could help you." The doctor was talking about the over-the-counter herb, Gingko Biloba, which can be found in every grocery store and is sold as a "memory enhancer."

Having nothing to lose—Gingko is natural, after all—I took it. And guess what? The entire problem was gone in four days! I still take it and have never looked back. This is the point when alternative medicine became legitimate for me. And this is when I came to understand how solutions can exist right under our noses, but we simply do not see these solutions because of how we are taught to think.

In this case, the doctor's training limited what he considered a legitimate healing solution. As the patient, I thought all high tech medicine had to be better than any low tech nutritional approach. We both had to change our belief structures and assumptions to get the outcome we needed. We both had to expand our definitions of what healing solutions look like. Sometimes it just boils down to doing what works, regardless of what you think.

> It ain't what you don't know that gets you into trouble. It's what you know for sure that just ain't so."
> —Mark Twain

Let's face it. Traditional medicine doesn't hold all the answers, and I'm the perfect example of that reality. Not so long ago about 50% of physicians did not believe autoimmune problems like Chronic Fatigue Syndrome and Fibromyalgia were even legitimate disease states. For those suffering with these conditions, I think you would agree that's a slap in the face.

This is an additional argument for giving complimentary medicine a chance. The art of medicine, like any other human endeavor, is subject to "Confirmation Bias" or what I call "Error Chains." Because it's human nature to defend a belief structure (such as accepted assumptions, industry norms), error chains sometimes develop around the diagnostic process and standards of care. The more an error is repeated, the less it is perceived to be an error. At some point the organizational dogma becomes very defensive about its belief structure, and that's the point at which you may need to step outside the traditional system. Such is the case when trying to integrate traditional with complimentary medicine. Realize that sometimes it might take a complete outsider to break an error chain in a diagnosis. And you are that outsider.

In short, the doctors who get insulted that you want a second opinion can be dangerous to your health, because their egos are tied up in their diagnoses and treatments. They are more hung up on being right than they are about your health. It is perfectly fine to fire an arrogant doctor. In fact, this is healthy, confident, and empowering behavior that will enable you to win the Inner Game of being a patient or a caregiver.

GOOD DECISION MAKING
BEGINS WITH GOOD QUESTIONS

Does the procedure, medicine, or therapy...?
      a) manage a symptom only
      b) get at the origin of the problem
      c) do both?

Am confident that I...?
      a) have the correct diagnosis
      b) am treating the problem with state of the art care

Do I feel that...?
      a) I am in the right place for my care
      b) I have left no stone unturned
      c) I have been well advised and made good decisions

Do I have a voice/input into my own healing process? Does the doc listen?

Are the providers sensitive to the emotional and spiritual impact of their medical care on me? Have they taken any steps to help me emotionally?

Do I have a process for finding some joy/happiness each day in spite of my circumstances?

Notes & Ideas

CHAPTER 7

Winning The Inner Game

> In every human endeavor there are two arenas of en-
> gagement: the outer and the inner. The outer game
> is played on an external arena to overcome external
> obstacles to reach an external goal. The inner game
> takes place within the mind of the player and is played
> against such obstacles as fear, self-doubt, lapses in focus,
> and limiting concepts or assumptions. The inner game
> is played to overcome the self-imposed obstacles...
>
> —Tim Gallaway, *The Inner Game of Tennis*

Winning the inner game of healthcare becomes a big battle for
our attention. Our intense focus on the adversity at hand is necessary but it is also the oxygen that feeds the emotional turmoil
that goes with it. HPPs and HPCGs are emotionally fit and flexible. Emotionally fit people are less inclined to allow their circumstance or their emotions define them. In short, they do not
allow their circumstance become their identity. They tend not to
get as consumed by events as easily as they did before. They don't

allow those sticky, contagious, emotional whirlwinds to steal their joy, which comes from within or from those around you. HPPs and HPCGs learn how to go deep into a peaceful state below the surface turbulence of adversity. Creating a sense of peace and calm is a skill that you too can learn.

> "…it's so important to look at addiction as being enslaved or in bondage to a belief system, a thought pattern, a paradigm, or simply a way of being."
>
> "…look at where you are spiritually, emotionally, and physically. And ask yourself: "Can I scare my way out of this? Can I be in fear enough to solve this problem? Have I done everything I can to solve this problem? Have I spoken to everyone I could speak to? Can I worry myself into healing? Can I suffer myself into healing?"
>
> —**Ester Nicholson**, *recovering addict for over 30 years*
> Vocalist (solo and with artists such as Rod Stewart and Bette Midler)
> Author, *Soul Recovery: 12 Keys to Healing Addiction* (www.soulrecovery.org)
> Excerpt from *Stories With A Purpose*

How do we get into a peaceful state? The first step is to create a space of stillness. This is where you check into the here and now. Learn to quiet your mind so you can hear and see opportunity. Unload the laundry list of "to-do's" that are running through your brain right now.

Begin by letting go of:

> All the complexity
> All the multi-tasking
> The excessive focus on the problem
> The technology
> Emotion in the past
> Anxiety in the future

Relax. Let go. Don't worry. The world will not fall apart in the next 15 minutes. A peaceful state happens when you are able to step outside the emotional identity, fear, intimidation, and turmoil of the circumstance long enough to reconnect with your core. This is where we need to be for healing and good decision making to occur.

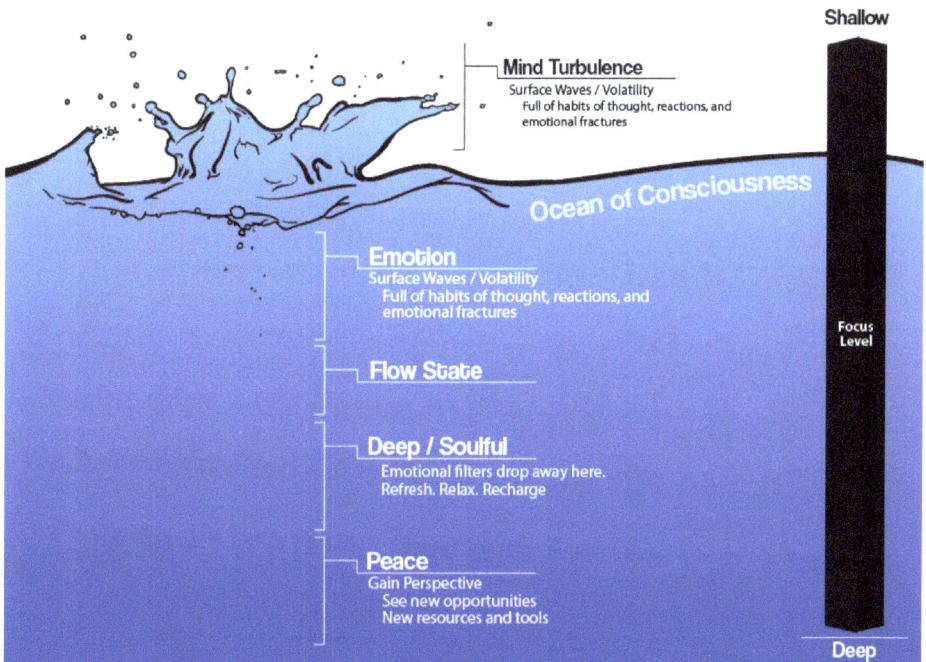

Most of us don't know we overcome powerful emotional storms with gratitude-driven, positive emotion. It is possible to reverse the flow of a downward emotional spiral into an upward, momentum-driven spiral. This skill is similar to turning into a skid, when your car is spinning on ice. It is also what pilots do when a plane stalls. They point the nose straight down so that they can pick up the air speed necessary to create lift and flight. Hard to believe but true that we can do this with our emotions. Flexing our gratitude muscle during a crisis is counter to what we think will help but, frankly, it is the single best way to get out of a downward emotional spiral.

This is how *The Opportunity Coach* works.

Relax:

Realize the emotion and the circumstance don't own you. You observe them from a state of mindful awareness. This is not avoidance of the emotion, but objective observation of it. Let go of the illusion of control, the illusion self-reliance, the excessive focus on the adversity.

Listen:

Discern opportunity during the chaos and turbulence. It is there. Seeing the opportunity is a matter of your state of mind and the questions you ask. Learn how to see through the eyes of gratitude. It is a skill. Trusting your instinct requires you to listen to your soul, not the outside circumstances that steal your attention.

Play:

When you know the turbulence of emotion and circumstance don't own you, you feel a great sense of freedom. Have some fun in the midst of the turmoil. Humor works. Celebrate! Remember the things that feed your soul and do them again. The art of play is curative.

Notes & Ideas

CHAPTER 8

Blinded by Abundance

About five years ago, my wife's cousin came from communist Cuba and moved in with us in our affluent area in Texas. She was accompanied by her husband and two daughters. The culture shock was tremendous. After living in Havana on around $100 per month for nearly forty years, they finally arrived in the land of plenty—or so we thought.

I will never forget our first visit as a family to the grocery store in our neighborhood. They stood at the entrance of the sliding glass doors and peered into the vast array of food displayed before them. I could hardly wait to see them jump for joy and celebrate that vast abundance we wanted to share. Before them were twelve versions of corn flakes and thirty types of breads. Who could want more?

Much to my surprise, the four simply turned around and walked back into the parking lot, overwhelmed, confused, and dejected. There were simply too many choices. They were discouraged, not empowered. What they saw was confusion, not opportunity.

They were trapped in an intellectual and emotional identity that was inflexible to any alternative other than the narrative they had in their heads. In short, they were blinded by abundance.

Like our cousins at the grocery store, most of us who are facing a health crisis have a huge set of tools, resources, and relationships all around us, but we may see only confusion, not opportunity. It is very common to be blinded by abundance in most healthcare and insurance settings. Technology adds to the mix by creating a constant source of distraction. Blind and distracted is where most of us are most of the time. How do we overcome this tendency to see confusion over opportunity?

INSIGHT

Your brain will see what you tell it to look for. A thankful frame of mind enables and activates our discernment of abundance that would otherwise remain hidden by our natural tendency to validate what we don't have. We call this learning how to see.

Learning How to See

High Performance Patients are good at gathering allies around them. HPPs develop relationships with a wide variety of people they run into in the course of their care like nurses, pharmacists, or nutritionists, whose collective wisdom can change the quality of their experience for the better. Most of the time these are informal relationships but it is amazing how many people want to help you if you give them an opportunity.

Here is what my caregiving "team" looked like:
Oncologist, Spouse, Cousins who are MDs, Friends and clients who are MDs, Surgical nurses, Physical Therapist, Nutritionist,

Pharmacist, Hypnotist, Psychologist, Care Coordination Team at Humana, Co-worker/rock climber, Prayer warriors, and probably a bunch of others I can't remember. In some way or another, they all contributed to a successful outcome.

To identify these people as a resource for you, we first need to start with the easy stuff. Let's begin by recognizing some right now. Fill out the *Constellation of Opportunity* form below to see what you have to work with today. There are probably more tools and relationships at your disposal than you think. This is where we may see opportunity in the form of relationships, tools, or resources we had overlooked. Remember, even the smallest advantage is something upon which you can build. Use everything at your disposal.

_____ Family Members
_____ MD & Specialist
_____ Nurses
_____ Patient Advocacy: Broker-Friends
_____ Complementary Medicine Provider
_____ Wellness Coach
_____ Pharmacist
_____ Fitness Instructor
_____ Co-Workers
_____ Insurance Carrier
_____ EAP Provider
_____ Price Shopping Service
_____ HSA / FSA / HRA: Vendor—TPA
_____ Voluntary Benefits Company
_____ Web-based Patient Communities

Notes & Ideas

CHAPTER 9

Climbing the Resilience Ladder

> ### INSIGHT
> *Adversity is, sometimes, the contrast we need to see. As darkness is necessary to see the stars, adversity forces us into a new perspective. Whether we know it or not, it is our choice to focus on either the darkness or the stars.*

Resilience and emotional flexibility are mostly abstract concepts and improvised processes, commonly known as "having guts" or "digging deep." Most of what we learn about resilience is from a coach or tough love parent, who told us simply to "suck it up." When confronted with a major medical challenge, these terms simply don't do much good, because they do not show how to be resilient.

Real resilience is not a coping mechanism. It is an improvisational art, which is very active and deliberate, and resilient patients can frequently improve outcomes. In those situations where a medical outcome cannot be changed, a resilient person can always improve the experience of their situation.

And this takes us full circle back to the difference between healing and curing. Healing works from the inside out. It begins with your spirit, your soul, or your emotional identity. Resilient people take control of their emotional and spiritual healing first and work from the inside to the outside. Understood this way, healing is always in our hands, not the doctor's hands. Our job is to meet the doctor working at curing disease from the outside-in. This is how HPPs set the stage for the science of medical care to be most effective.

The two most important abilities of high performance patients are:

- The ability to reframe an event as an opportunity to expand our personal growth and freedom, or as an opportunity to express our purpose.
- The ability to discern even the smallest opportunity in chaos and confusion upon which we can build.

How do HPPs and HPGCs make this happen? They ask good questions like:

- What do I notice about what is going on around me right now?
- What can I learn from this adversity?
- What do I need to let go of?
- What have I overlooked?
- What do I need to value more?

Here is the profile of a typical HPP or HPCG. You too can get here.

Profile Of
High Performance Patients
and
High Performance Caregivers

* Are "situationally aware" and pay attention to details *

* Reframe adversity as growth opportunities *

* Build on the small successes *

* Conserve energy and let go of battles out of their control *

* Become comfortable with contradictions *

* Use gratitude to emotionally live above circumstances *

* Challenge assumptions and learn to say "No" *

* Disregard boundaries and rules that do not serve a purpose *

* Become bigger emotional risk-takers *

* Tap into their soul/core/purpose and God regularly *

And here is what the typical progression toward resilience looks like for both the patient and the caregiver. Don't forget caregivers, sometimes, suffer more than the patient, so this same learning curve will apply equally to them.

Phase 1
Crushed and Hyper-Compliant
Stripped of self-image, follow rules, regardless of impact on self. Most of us begin here, hyper-compliant to externals, ignoring our internal voice.

Phase 2
Coping and Quietly Selective
Making it day to day, marginally functional, being a "patient" patient. Dare to set boundaries. Quietly integrate alternative care into your traditional care regime, without telling your doctor. Begin to tune in and believe what our bodies are telling us. Start to limit blind compliance to an external set of rules, protocols, and assumptions. You begin to feel emotionally better.

Phase 3
Empowered and Healthy Non-Compliance
You feel in control—balance physical care with quality of life, as determined by you, the patient. Question assumptions. You are assertive. You are, now, equally guided by your instinct and external realities. You are engaged in the process.

Phase 4
Transformed—My Mess Becomes My Mission
Living above the circumstance, winning the emotional battle, independent of physical. Trauma is transformed into purpose. You can help others and that heals you.

Meet my friend Carlos Gonzalez—poster-child of adaptive be-havior and patient resiliency. He is from Mexico and was born with severe case of cerebral palsy—a circumstance that most peo-ple would consider highly limiting. Carlos left the warm climate of Mexico for cold Canada, where he knew no one, did not speak English well, and had no job, friends, or family. Carlos went there to challenge himself and his ability to live and work inde-pendently. He now has a job, learned English, and helps others through a local cerebral palsy non-profit. But most impressively Carlos plays ice hockey for fun. Carlos and many other like him are part of the "I Am Adaptive" movement. They are an inspira-tion to us all and remind us what life is really all about. You go Carlos!

Notes & Ideas

CHAPTER 10

The Wisdom of Survivors

We have found that resilient and adaptive people are all around us. They are everyday heroes whose incredible stories are trapped in silos of personal experience. Most of these people are humble and don't believe that their stories are unusual or instructive. I challenge you to tap into those stories and you will notice how resilient people are able to take an extreme amount of adversity and redirect the power of that adversity in their favor. They don't necessarily avoid pain or suffering, but they are able to infuse adversity with:

- A mission or purpose
- An expansion of their own freedom
- A growth opportunity
- And in some cases, all three

Have you ever wondered why some survivors say their trauma was a "blessing?" The answer is these people use the adversity as a "Take 2" in life and they dramatically increase the quality of their lives. When adversity makes you remember what feeds your soul, it can be transformative. The mistake most of us make in life is waiting for the life clock to run down before we begin living our "bucket list." Sometimes the adversity you have in front of you is your opportunity to get moving on your life's mission now.

On a SWAP show I did recently I asked a young 16-year-old Ryan Barry and his 18-year-old sister Kaitlin why they felt "blessed" by the limits of Cystic Fibrosis, I was told:

> "With my Cystic Fibrosis diagnosis at birth and the lifestyle it demands, I have to live in a constant state of awareness of a higher power, instead of a constant focus on myself. And this changes the quality of my life."

For me this is an astounding life lesson from two very young but very wise people. These two have created a new definition of strength which acknowledges and even celebrates their physical weakness because it puts them in a perfect position to receive emotional and spiritual strength. They have learned the art of God-reliance, not self-reliance and that is ultimately the key to transforming adversity into purposeful living.

Knowing all this, my question for you is: Why wait for a trauma, adversity, or illness to begin to dramatically improve the quality of life, when you can learn what wisdom looks like right now?

Time becomes more important than money.
They stop playing life too safe.
They recall what used to make them happy, and they begin
    doing it again.
They simplify and declutter their lives.
They give more and take less.
They repair broken relationships and forgive.
They get rid of toxic relationships.
They listen for direction and discern their purpose.
They decide to live a life of impact.
They are the most grateful people around.

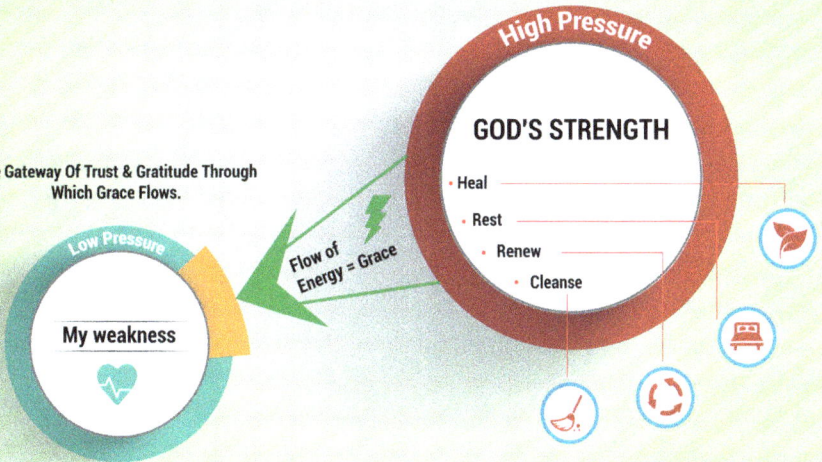

LEARNING HOW TO RECEIVE

Spiritual Physics For High Performance Patients

High Pressure

GOD'S STRENGTH

- Heal
- Rest
- Renew
- Cleanse

The Gateway Of Trust & Gratitude Through Which Grace Flows.

Low Pressure

Flow of Energy = Grace

My weakness

Notes & Ideas

PART II
SMART MONEY

CHAPTER 11

Introduction to Smart Money
Becoming an Empowered Healthcare Consumer

Part II Smart Money is part of this book, designed to change the financial experience you have as a patient, or "healthcare consumer." As a patient, I realized the delivery of excellent medical care is quite different from the experience we have paying for it.

As an insurance professional, you would think I'd be the patient with no problem navigating the financial and insurance elements of our healthcare system, right? Wrong! The administrative and financial segments of our structure don't like to acknowledge gaps, miscommunication, high error rates, incompetence, complexity, egos, or unsustainable costs; rather, it is a system that begs for help, guidance, and advocacy.

Our vision is to give you the tools, leverage, and confidence you need to make our healthcare system responsive to you as an empowered healthcare consumer. Shouldn't healthcare be about the patient, not the doctor or the insurance company?

The difficulties don't lie exclusively with you and me; these financial obstacles are equally hostile for employees of doctors' offices, insurance companies, and hospital staff. Virtually everyone is exposed to this massive, chronic, and widespread problem.

What does the average person do?

What you can do is ask **powerful questions** that may save your money AND your life, such as:

- Can you remind me WHY am I taking this particular prescription, again?
- Why are we doing this MRI?
- How can I do this naturally?
- How can I make payments to you?
- What if we waited on this surgery?

Identifying The Problem

Here's the deal: Healthcare is a system that takes control of our wallets *if we let it happen*. And, boy, do we. Why? Because we've been taught:

good patient = passive patient

**passive patient =
doesn't question healthcare plans or cost**

This old-school mentality tells us outcomes for our health and for our wallets are out of our control, but that's not true.

Let's examine a commonly held misconception:

MISCONCEPTION
The copays we pay represent
the total cost of medical care.

This couldn't be further from the truth!

Did you know the "$35 baby" costs about $7,000+ to deliver?
We just never saw the bill.

For years, every procedure, test, prescription, and service has been paid for in full by somebody—an insurance company or an employer. But that cost is increasingly being shifted to you and me. The days of paying $35 to deliver a baby in your HMO are gone.

NEWS FLASH
While we want to give doctors control over our medical situation, we don't want to cede control over our wallets. It's our job, as patients, to control the cost, not the medical providers, but it's highly likely no one ever told you this.

DEFINING "COST SHIFT"
Have you heard these words: "This year, our deductibles are going up," or "This year our premiums went up"?

Why is this happening?
Because most players in the healthcare system have no incentive to pay attention to prices.

There are no incentives for patients to be cost conscious if they have fixed copays. Who cares what the real cost of any service is, when the cost to you is limited to a $25 copay? Add to that the fact doctors not only don't know the cost of the medical care they provide, but they don't *want* to know. Why? Because they're taught that cost and pricing might bias their medical recommendations.

> **INSIGHT**
> Realize your doctors are not trained to know the cost of anything. This doesn't mean they're bad doctors; rather, it means they focus on your health, irrespective of the price.

I told you previously that the cost of healthcare is going up at an unsustainable rate. But we will not try to tackle in this book if this is right or wrong or who is at fault; it is what it is, so let's make it our starting point.

★ **Government does not control the cost; they merely shift cost to taxpayers. The result is higher prices.** ★
★ **Political wrangling occurs.** ★
★ **Your company must deal with the reality of annual increases.** ★
★ **Financial realities spawned a movement, called Consumer Driven Health Care, which commands your attention.** ★

> *If you put the federal government in charge of the Sahara Desert, in five years, there'd be a shortage of sand.*
> —**Milton Friedman,** Nobel Prize-winning economist

WHAT IS CONSUMER DRIVEN HEALTHCARE?

Consumer driven plans are a new way of saying we will apply all the simple, common-sense rules of frugal shopping to the world of healthcare. When shopping for food, cars, appliances, and electronics, what do we do?

- We shop for both quality and price.
- We know the cost of something before we buy it.
- We take control of our wallets.
- We ask lots of questions.
- We negotiate.

If you've been introduced to a consumer driven plan, or you are trying to learn if it's right for you, or you are hearing about it for the first time, you're in the right place! And even if you have no classic consumer driven health plan, for example, if you do not have an HSA, you'll still want to pay attention, because any health plan where you incur a large deductible expense is a big incentive to become a Smart Patient. All the same principles will apply.

INSIGHT

We, as consumers, are caught in a financial Twilight Zone, which has become a tug-of-war between government-controlled healthcare pricing and free-market forces battling it out for our money. It's not a conflict we become aware of until we have a big medical bill or an insurance policy that puts our money at risk up front.

Then, and only then, do we pay attention.

HOW DOES A CONSUMER DRIVEN PLAN WORK?

Costs drive our behavior. It's human nature to be more careful with our own money than we are with somebody else's. When our own hard-earned dollars are at stake, we are more cost conscious. When enough people become cost-conscious consumers, the prices for everybody go down. It's only through the process of healthcare consumers flexing their muscles will the cost of care decrease. The government is not coming to the rescue; it's you and I demanding change as consumers who will make a difference. Collectively, we have power!

Health insurance policies that adopt this "skin-in-the-game" philosophy are called "consumer driven." Any plan where you have to deal with out-of-pocket costs requires you to be a good consumer. Why? Because you care about where the money goes. However, there is a new generation of product:

Health Savings Accounts
High-deductible health plans that are attached to bank accounts.
We call them HSA plans for short.

Why would I want an HSA?

HSAs and other consumer driven insurance plans are different for most of us, who have been in HMOs or rich "copay plans" that cover every sniffle. But here's the benefit:

INSIGHT
Consumer Driven Plans Are *Less Expensive.*
In addition, they put *Responsibility* and *Control* back in *our hands.*

How much less expensive? These plans can cost 20% less than traditional plans—**20% less**! (and that could be the amount of a car payment for some of you!) Also, the rate of increase on these plans, year after year, is lower and less rapid, so our employer will promote these plans, too.

WHAT DO WE DO NOW?

Let's make it simple. You need only to adopt two characteristics:

Be Assertive and Be Resourceful.

Why are these qualities important for you?

They allow you to:
- Recognize a threat to your wallet exists.
- Take responsibility for your own health and finances.
- Use common sense and do your homework.
- Become your own best advocate.
- Form a team with those who can help you navigate the system.

Reversing the Flow

Passive Patient
- **Unaware**
- **Unconfident**
- **Dependent**
- **Out of Control**

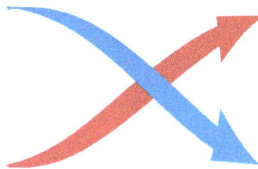

Smart Patient
- **Power**
- **Confident**
- **Control**
- **Aware**

Notes & Ideas

CHAPTER 12

Part One: Health Insurance 101— Insider Tips on the Basics

Having given hundreds of group health insurance review meetings, I've learned it's always best to begin with a review of the basics—what I call Health Insurance 101. Even in the most sophisticated groups in the healthcare profession, inevitably, somebody learns something of value, and that tidbit almost always saves money.

INSIDER TIPS THAT WILL KEEP YOU SMART

Plan Design

Deductibles for the vast majority of you reset on January 1.
Consolidate all medical bills in the same calendar year. This is critical when timing an elective medical procedure.

Preventive care is covered in all plans at 100%.
No copays or deductibles. It's free so get your annual physical!

The lowest deductible does not always equate to the best health plan.

Higher deductibles mean lower premiums. Eighty-five percent of the time, you won't pay your deductible anyway, why spend a lot of extra money to have a low deductible?

> ### TRY THIS:
> Buy a lower-cost HSA plan and put the savings in your own pre-tax HSA account to pay the expenses when you need it. Think of it this way: The lower-cost HSA plans will generate savings to you. Then your biggest question is: What do I do with the savings? You can either send the money to the insurance company for a lower-deductible plan, or you can put it into your own pre-tax bank account.
> Which would you rather do?

Shopping

Know the price of a procedure before you "buy" it.
Did you know prices for medical services frequently vary by 300–500%, even when using In-Network services? Shop these prices, especially on items that will hit your deductible. You wouldn't buy a car and let them bill you after they deliver it to you (or if you would do that, then you probably wouldn't be reading this right now). Why would you do that for your healthcare?

Use technology—Internet and phone—to compare doctors and pricing.
You've probably heard of the *Kelly Blue Book*, right? It's the resource that tells you how much a used car is worth. Well, did you know there's a healthcare version? Go to www.healthcarebluebook.com to shop the price of medical procedures by zip code. It's free and will educate you on what services should cost. If you're being charged too much, flex your

consumer muscles and find another provider or buy a service that does the shopping for you, such as Dallas-based Compass at www.compassphs.com

Always confirm your doctor is In-Network.

The *exact* name of the network is on your ID card, so you don't need to remember.

Alternative medicine may still save money, even if not covered by insurance.

Sometimes, you can solve a problem non-surgically with a process, like deep tissue massage or homeopathic and nutritional remedies such as herbs or organic foods, saving you thousands of dollars, lots of time, and improving your quality of life.

Billing/Payments

Know that providers frequently negotiate bills and payment plans.

If you don't ask, they won't tell you (we're talking about bills $500 and up).

Negotiate a deductible down payment.

Go for a "down payment" of 20% of your deductible.

Insurance companies send an Explanation of Benefits (EOB), not actual bills.

An EOB explains the discounts they're applying to your medical procedure. Suggestion: Register online with your insurance carrier, so you can get your EOB immediately—no waiting for snail mail.

Pay no bill until you know for certain you owe it.

EOBs from insurance companies and provider bills are not co-ordinated and can easily have crossover—your doctor may have been paid, but they send you a bill, anyway. It's possible you don't owe it or may only owe a portion of the bill. Know that hospitals have a 50% error rate on bills sent directly to you. Your insurance carrier tracks what you owe.

How do I find out?

Call your insurance company—they keep close watch on what you owe versus what they owe. Remember, they're on the hook for the bills, and believe me, they keep track. Call them and go over the EOB to see what you owe. It might save you a lot of money!

Case in Point
Billing from Bangalore, India

I had a cardiology group as a client of my insurance brokerage company for several years, who hired a third-party service in India to send bills to their patients. They wanted to cut some of the administrative overhead for their business, which was great for them, but not so good for their patients. Do you think there was any coordination between the cardiology group, their billing company in India, and the insurance company?

Unfortunately, no.

The result was the cardiology group may have already been paid for the procedure by the patient's insurance company, but the patient got the bill, anyway. This is precisely why you need to pay close attention to your bills—you don't want to send your doctor money for a bill for which they've already been paid!

A high percentage of doctors, hospitals, and providers of all types hire third-party billing companies, who crank out invoices faster than the Federal Reserve prints money.

Remember:

INSIGHT
Never pay a bill until you know you actually owe it.

Don't go to the Emergency Room for non-emergencies.
Save the ER for life- or limb-threatening emergencies. Urgent situations belong in walk-in Urgent Care clinics, where you receive a big savings, compared to the ER.

Try Telemedicine (a doc on the phone or Internet).
Telemedicine companies offer 24/7/365 access to primary care MDs for a wide range of basic needs. You can stay at home or work, call on the phone, or communicate by Internet, and they can write a prescription when the situation calls for it. It saves time and money! Telemedicine is rapidly becoming a major trend; now is the time to get used to it.

Part Two: Health Savings Accounts 101—Universal Rules You Need to Know

GENERAL INFO

HSA Plans have two parts:

1. The HSA account is what you call the *bank account*.
2. The High-Deductible Health Plan (HDHP) is what you call the *insurance*.

   Bank Account + HDHP = HSA Plan

THE INSURANCE PART

- There are no copays for doctor visits or prescriptions.
- All preventive care is covered without cost.
- Every expense is counted toward your deductible.
- You pay bills, until total deductible is reached; after that, the insurance company pays.
- You pay the "wholesale" price—In-Network discount rate—for medical services (up to 60% off retail, a rate insurance companies have negotiated for you).

THE BANK ACCOUNT PART (THE HEALTH SAVINGS ACCOUNT)

- Your deposits are tax-free.
- Employer deposits are tax-free.
- What you don't spend during the year, you keep!
- You can use the money on any dependent in your family, not just on your expenses.
- Money can be used on anything that is *medically necessary*, even some procedures not covered by the health plan, such as dental expenses, prescription glasses, diabetic supplies, etc.

- You, not your employer, must open the account.
- You must open the account *before* you incur any medical expense.
- It is your personal bank account and goes with you if you change jobs.
- It's designed to be a long-term, pre-tax savings tool.
- At age 65, the restrictions on using the money only for medical expenses disappear; savings become like an IRA.
- If you move back to a plan that's not an HSA, you can deposit no more money into the HSA bank account, but you can continue to use the money in the account on qualified medical expenses.

The IRS limits on pre-tax contributions are:

Year	Single	Family
2015	$3,350	$6,650
2016	$3,350	$6,750

* More than one person is considered a family for these calculations.

** If you are 55 years or older, you can add $1,000 to these IRS limits.

NOTE:

To be eligible for an HSA health plan, you must:

- not be enrolled in Medicare Part A or Part B
- have a valid social security number and U.S. residence
- not be covered by Tri-Care
- not have accessed VA benefits in the past 90 days

Notes & Ideas

CHAPTER 13

Three Key Ways to Save Money and Get the Care You Deserve

There are three major ways to save money as healthcare consumers and, believe it or not, most of us focus on one and forget the other two. But being a Smart Patient means taking advantage of all three. The total cost of healthcare is a combination of insurance premiums (paid by your employer and by you) and your actual out-of-pocket costs (co-pays, deductibles, co-insurance). You are also entitled to discounts, negotiated by your insurance provider. Think of investing in your health, where you want to optimize spending for benefits, and your return on investment includes both better health and savings realized from your historical and current spending habits. Here's how you can garner the most savings across the board.

LOWER YOUR MONTHLY OUTLAY FOR INSURANCE
Choosing the right plan is key and ensures two things:

1. You won't be overpaying for coverage.
2. You won't take on more risk than you can handle.

People often ignore the price of insurance, causing them to buy a health plan that exceeds their needs. Why buy a Cadillac convertible when your necessities can be met with a reliable Toyota truck? Payroll deductions for your health insurance keep rising. It's time to pay attention to the price.

MANAGE YOUR FAMILY'S HEALTH BETTER

Common sense tells us that staying healthy costs less for everybody. But most of us aren't aware that 67% of *all* medical costs are associated with problems we create ourselves.

Here are a few prime examples:

- Chronic stress leads to high blood pressure and triggers numerous autoimmune diseases.
- Smoking promotes cardiovascular problems and cancer (and the cigarettes, themselves, are costing you a bundle).
- Weight issues cause cardio and joint problems, as well as diabetes.

No doubt, you've heard all this before, but hopefully you're more aware of how costs are linked to your lifestyle choices. If your company offers a Wellness Plan, join it and participate in the incentives they offer, because your lifestyle choices will cost you more money otherwise.

The
SPA Profile

S — **Save 3 Ways**
- Buy the right amount of insurance
- Stay Healthy
- Learn how to use Insurance

P — **Partner with your MD**
- You play an equal part in your health as your MD
- You assemble the pieces of the healthcare puzzle for your MD
- You question and negotiate
- You control your medical records

A — **Aware of the Dangers and Opportunities**
- MD's don't know the price of anything
- 300%-500% price differentials for the same procedure
- You may not owe THAT bill
- You may benefit for a blend of traditional & alternative procedures
- Your MD may not be in network
- Learn your hospital safety scores

HOW YOU USE YOUR INSURANCE CAN SAVE YOU BIG $$

You are in the driver's seat and Smart Patient Academy is your driver's education class!

- Shop for medical providers, based on cost and quality. Learn to minimize the impact of deductibles or avoid them altogether.
- Tell the doctor what procedures you're comfortable paying for.
- Negotiate large medical bills into smaller ones.
- Create payment plans with doctors.
- Use pre-tax dollars on healthcare expenses.
- Utilize telemedicine to save time and money for routine primary care.

- Incorporate complementary, or alternative, medicine to treat problems where traditional medicine favors invasive surgical procedures or medicines with many side effects.

Not sure how to use the above tips? Not to worry! This is the essence of becoming a Smart Patient. We're going to break this down in the subsequent chapters so that you'll learn how to save money like a champ!

Notes & Ideas

CHAPTER 14

Are You In-Network?
What's a Network Again?

In the insurance business, one of the most common problems we work to resolve for our clients concerns the use of doctors "In-Network" versus those "Out-of-Network."

I know. We talk about "Networks" and assume everybody knows what that means. For those who are unclear:

> **DEFINITION**
> A **Network** is the list of medical providers you should use within your plan.

Yes, it's that simple. In most plans, you can go "Out-of-Network" to get care, but you will pay a much higher price for that care than you would "In-Network."

Note: Insurance companies used to give you a big book of network providers, but now they maintain the list on the company website.

Remember, it is your responsibility as a Smart Patient to confirm the doctor you're using is In-Network. How do you do this? Simple: **check online; after that, verify their listing by phone or in person.** Why? Because a doctor's practice is an independent business, and they can alter their contracts with the insurance network at almost any time. This makes the network list of providers a constantly changing entity.

Here's the critical reason to ask if your doctor is In-Network:

If a doctor tells you they're In-Network and it turns out they're not, the fact you were misinformed shifts the responsibility for the bill to *them*, not you.

This misguidance on the doctor's part transfers the liability to the doctor and away from *you*. With a surgery, that detail can mean thousands of dollars you're not liable to pay!

Here are some additional points you'll want to have for reference:

A life-threatening emergency is considered In-Network, regardless of where you are.
Note: Life-threatening means you think you're dying or losing a limb. A hangover is *not* an emergency.

Always show your ID card to the receptionist, so they can identify the exact name of the network you're in.
Why? Aetna and Humana have about 20+ networks each! If you simply ask, "Do you take Aetna?" the answer could be, "Yes," but that may not apply to the specific Aetna network *you* are in. Your card will help discern if you're within a covered network.

To get the most out of insurance policies, you need to utilize the In-Network doctors on the list.

Why? A large part of the premiums we pay for insurance goes toward buying big discounts—which is one of our most valuable benefits—from the doctors, hospitals, and all other In-Network providers.

Be clear you expect all providers during a surgery to be In-Network.

This ensures that if the In-Network surgeon invites an Out-of-Network anesthesiologist or fellow surgeon to assist, the liability for the extra cost is on the doctor, not you. Clarify, up front, what you expect.

You're becoming a smarter patient by the minute! Now that we've tackled networks, let's get those deductibles figured out!

Notes & Ideas

CHAPTER 15

When Do I Pay My Deductible Again?
Which Is Best, How Much, and Why

Confusion surrounding deductibles is the most common source of questions I'm asked in a benefits enrollment meeting. Whether it wasn't explained well the first time or it's just plain confusing, people need clarification on this topic. Let's take out the confusion, once and for all.

> **DEFINITION**
> The **deductible** is the amount you pay 100% out of your pocket, before insurance is applied to your expenses.

A word on Preventive Care: As of January 2011, all health plans offer Preventive Care at 100%, without deductibles or copays, using In-Network doctors. That takes the cost off your shoulders for your annual physical, well-woman exams, and vaccinations for the kids.

You no longer must worry about these in relation to your deductible, so you've lost all excuses for tending to your annual health-maintenance visits. Translation: Get your physical!

Note: Double check that the visit will be "coded" as preventive care; otherwise, you might be in for a surprise bill, when you thought the exam and related tests would be free.

The cases when you pay a deductible depend upon the plan you have. Let's simplify.

SCENARIO 1—THE COPAY PLAN

You're on a plan *with* office visit copays.
Remember: *A copay is a known price you pay for a medical service, unrelated to your deductible.*
This much you know:

★ See the doctor ★

★ Pay your fixed copay ★

★ Incur no further expenses ★

When does the deductible kick in?

You will incur a deductible bill when you're *outside a doctor's office* getting healthcare. This occurs when you need:

- Inpatient hospital care
- Outpatient surgery
- Outpatient diagnostic (labs, X-rays, MRI, etc.)
- Emergency room care
- Ambulance transport

If you're in these circumstances, you will most likely incur a deductible expense; otherwise, your copay covers your basic visit.

THE GOOD NEWS

About 85% of you on this plan will never incur a deductible expense, because you will only see the doctor in their office and then get a prescription, for which you'll have copays.

Bottom line: **Most in Scenario #1 will not reach your deductible during a "normal" year.** The fixed copays are your only out-of-pocket expense, which makes the fear of a $2,500 deductible less daunting, as your odds of reaching it are small.

Important exception to this rule:

Dermatologists, Ear Nose and Throat doctors (ENTs), and Cardiologists are notorious for office visits that turn into impromptu "outpatient surgical procedures" or other diagnostic procedures that don't fit under a doctor visit copay. You know that mole the dermatologist removed? That was an outpatient surgery, with a $250 deductible hit. When in doubt, ask before they do the procedure!

SCENARIO 2—THE HSA (HEALTH SAVINGS ACCOUNT) PLAN

You're on a high-deductible health plan with *no* office visit copays.
Again, all preventive care is covered at 100%, so you incur no cost there. But, for the rest of the services you require, *your out-of-pocket expenses will go toward your deductible **all** of the time.* This is called, "self-insuring for the amount of your deductible." When does insurance help? After you've paid out your total deductible.

⋆ See the doctor or buy a prescription ⋆

⋆ Pay the wholesale price of the visit/procedure/drug (except for preventive care—remember this is covered by insurance, no matter what) ⋆

⋆ Payment goes toward deductible ⋆

⋆ After deductible is reached, insurance pays for all further medical expenses ⋆

Important Note:
Some good news is you will only owe the doctor the *negotiated* rate—or rather, the discounted rate, pre-negotiated by your insurance carrier. These discounts can be from 10%–60%. You're paying a wholesale price for the services under the HSA plan.

> *But wait! I pay $2,500*
> *before I get any benefit of insurance?*
>
> *Why on earth would anybody want to do this?*

When the premium (amount you pay annually for your plan) is 30%+ cheaper for you and your family, it looks attractive, because *you keep the money, instead of sending it to your insurance company.* The premium savings may be much more than you must spend on doctor visits during the year. If you do not use healthcare often, this plan may be a smarter move.

In addition, your employer may deposit money into your HSA account to help offset your deductible, a deposit that is not taxable to you. It may be hard to believe, but it's true!

EXAMPLE

Expensive Copay Plan:
$1,000 Deductible = $2,700 Annual Premium

Inexpensive HSA Plan:
$2,500 Deductible = $1,200 Annual Premium

Both could cost you $3,700 total if you pay a deductible, plus your premium; however, if you have no expenses that go toward your deductible, you'll save $1,500 up front, per year, with the lower-premium HSA plan. The best fit boils down to the risk you're comfortable taking.

Remember what we said initially? The best plan for you is not necessarily the one with the lowest deductible. It depends on how you use healthcare in a normal year and how much you're being charged.

Now, let's look at which plan is the best fit for you!

Notes & Ideas

CHAPTER 16

Which Plan Is Best for Me?
Simple Ways to Help You Decide

Isn't it great to know our insurance is right for us?

The insurance industry has spent the last twenty years training consumers to believe the lower the deductible, the better the plan. This is the old HMO mentality (remember, you used to pay $10 for an office visit copay, and the new baby cost $35). This was a great plan, except we forgot to ask what this wonderful arrangement cost in premium. However, now some of the premium cost has been shifted to you and me, so we've paid attention.

> ### DEFINITION
> The **Premium** is the amount you pay annually for your health insurance plan.

When we figure in premium cost, the $10 copay plan might not look so good. To make a sound decision and match the right insurance to your personal situation, the first thing you have to know is:

WHAT KIND of HEALTHCARE CONSUMER AM I?

Johnny Marvelous

Average Alex

Disaster Man

· Generic RX Primarily
· Spends less than $500/yr
· Sees MD 3x/yr

· Name Brand RX Only
· Spending $1000-$3000/yr
· Specialist 2-3/yr

· Chronic Medical Problem
· Spending $3000/yr or more
· Sees Multiple Specialists
· Big Surgery Pending

A.   Super-Healthy (80% of you)

The "I rarely/never go to the doctor" person

- Spends $500 or less out-of-pocket on medical expenses per year
- Goes to the doctor 3 or fewer times a year and gets an annual physical
- Takes generic medications only (if any)

B.   Middle of the Road (15% of you)

The "Yeah, I'm healthy, but need my maintenance meds" person

- May take maintenance medications for varied chronic underlying issues, but is healthy, otherwise, and rarely misses work
- Spends $1,000–$3,000 per year on medical expenses; most are associated with name-brand drugs for which there are no generic equivalents
- Sees specialists 3 times a year or more

## C.	Disaster Man/Woman (5% of you)

The "You bet I use my insurance!" person

- May have ongoing, long-term conditions, like diabetes or autoimmune diseases; impending, short-term elective surgeries, like a knee replacement or baby delivery; or perhaps is just an accident-prone, sick person.
- Spends over $3,000 a year on medical expenses
- Sees multiple specialists each year for various problems
- Has skateboarding, bronco-riding, rock-climbing children, who end up in the ER fre-quently

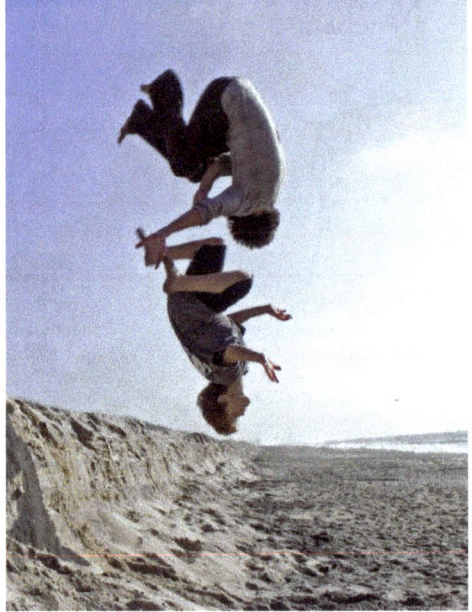

Hmm…Emergency Room or Urgent Care Center?

Once we know where we fit, we can choose a plan that corresponds to our medical needs. Our goal is to buy the right insurance—not too much and not too little.

What's interesting is you'll find Ms. Healthy and Disaster Man should often buy the same plan.

So, let's do some simple math. I promise; it's simple.

FINANCIAL ANALYSIS

Most of us are confronted with two health plan choices, where we're asked to compare a "Copay Plan" to an "HSA Plan" with no copays, then we're asked to choose. But how do you know which plan is best for you? To answer this question, you need to know three things:

1. What does my insurance cost me each year in premiums?
2. What is the most I would pay for a huge medical bill this calendar year?
3. Is my employer putting any money into my HSA bank account? (If you have no HSA, the answer is $0.)

Find out:
- What you pay annually (your premium) for your insurance.
- How much you would pay for healthcare in a worst-case scenario.
- How much your employer puts into your HSA.

Even if your financial analysis points to an HSA plan as the best fit for you, there's one more important factor to consider, before making your final decision:

Will I be happy in this plan?

Here's what we mean:

HSA upside: Has lower premiums and will max out the plan deductible faster.

HSA downside: Doctors, hospitals, and pharmacists owe you a discount as network providers, but will not know exactly what to charge you at the point of service. This can be a hassle and, sometimes, that hassle factor is not worth the premium savings. It depends on the personality of the consumer.

EXAMPLE

Let's say, you (or your spouse) are a new stay-at-home mom/dad. Taking a crying baby to the doctor with an earache is hard enough, but to do so without knowing the price or having to negotiate a bill can cause a lot of unnecessary frustration. We don't want you spending your premium savings on antidepressants. If you envision yourself in this scenario, go with the copay plan; the extra cost of your premium will be worth it. You can always change your plan next year, when circumstances change.

To summarize, here's a guide for who best benefits from each plan:

Copay Plan HSA Plan

You have:	You are:
Mid-range health / High Rx usage	Very healthy or very sick
Immediate access to copays	Aggressive saver and shopper

You prefer:	You prefer:
Easier cash-flow management	Insurance as safety net
No price shopping required	An additional savings vehicle
No budgeting/savings required	Negotiating medical bills

Armed with knowledge of which plan suits you and/or your family's needs best, let's take the confusion out of prescriptions, so you'll never pay too much for them again!

Notes & Ideas

CHAPTER 17

Generic, Name Brand, and What's That Third Thing?
Removing the Mystery behind Rx Shopping

How do I avoid prescription drug sticker shock?

In virtually every training session I hold, somebody in the crowd gets an immediate savings. How? We simply explain the cost difference between a *name-brand* drug versus a *generic* one. For some of you, this is basic stuff, but if you haven't checked to see if there's a generic alternative for the name-brand drug you're taking, or if a "therapeutic alternative" may fit, you could pay hundreds of extra dollars you need not spend. Remember, name brands lose their patents all the time, which allows the competition to come in and copy the drug for a fraction of the cost. **Patients who take generic drugs could save up to 90% on their prescriptions.** If you're *not* clear on the difference, here's the important thing to know:

Generic Drug

The active ingredient (the medicine) has the exact same chemical makeup as the name brand; only the filler materials are different. The generic should work equally well, but not always. Any side effects from generics, typically, come from the filler materials.

Most plans have three drug categories. Most of us are only familiar with the first two: generic and name brand. The question arises: "Generic, name brand, and what's that third thing?"

The third category is what's called the Level-3 drug, sometimes referred to as "non-formulary," meaning no discounts.

What Is a Formulary?

The insurance company's menu of prescriptions covered by insurance. This menu classifies drugs into categories from least expensive to most expensive (1-3), so a Level 3 drug will be the most expensive.

Put into plain English, this means there are two or more name-brand drugs that do the same thing, and they compete. (You've seen those ads on TV, right? They're not selling the generic, nor the cheaper of the two competing name-brand drugs.) Your insurance company has negotiated a lower price for one name brand versus another and put them into their appropriate categories.

If I have two name-brand drugs, and they both do the same thing, why would I choose the Level-3 option, when I can get a Level-2 drug cheaper?

Let's use two names you've probably heard of:

For years, Lipitor has been a Level-2 drug that cost a $25 copay, and Zocor has, typically, been a level-3 drug that costs $50. The doctor doesn't care if you take Lipitor or Zocor but, remember, he also doesn't know the price of either. Their job is to pay attention to the medical outcome for the patient; our job is to pay attention to the price. But, because you're a Smart Patient and have done your homework, you've discovered Zocor has a generic equivalent called Simvastatin for $4.99, with or without a copay plan.

The question is: Why would you buy Lipitor or Zocor, when you can buy Simvastatin for $4.99 and get the same outcome? After checking with your doctor to be sure they approve, ask if a generic exists in the category of drugs being prescribed; otherwise, they might not remember to request it.

Note: If you're on an HSA plan with no copays, the price for Lipitor or Zocor ranges from $99/month to $120/month, depending on where you buy the drug. Having a generic alternative, like Simvastatin, could save you $100/month!

Here's your prescription (and this one's free!) for managing your prescription drug budget:

- Ask your doctor for a generic equivalent.
- Ask your doctor to write the prescription ("script") in a way that allows the pharmacist to find the lowest cost alternative on your insurance plan's formulary.
- Ask your doctor if there is a "therapeutic alternative" to the name-brand drug they're prescribing.
- Shop for scripts via the Internet to find the lowest prices (see Resources section).

- Many doctors are liberal in dispensing samples of name-brand drugs, given to them by the drug company salespeople. There is no charge for these samples and, frequently, the doctor will give you a 1–2 month supply. Always ask if they have samples you can try.
- Use mail-order service and buy a 90-day supply as needed. The cost is frequently lower when you buy higher quantities, by as much as 30%.
- If you must use a name-brand prescription, look for a manufacturer's coupon online. Some drug companies release coupons your pharmacy can apply to your prescription cost every month.
- Try pill-splitting. It is not uncommon to pay the same price for a 20-milligram prescription as it is for a 10-milligram. If your plan allows it, you may get a 20-milligram script and cut the pill in half, which gives you a 60-day supply for a 30-day price—a nifty 50% reduction in cost!

Flexing Our Consumer Muscle

You probably don't know prescriptions vary in price by location

...and the reason most people don't know, for example, Walgreens is the single most expensive place to buy a prescription, and places like Walmart or Costco are the cheapest is because they have a prescription card copay plan. Those Rx copays shield us from knowing the true cost of the medicine, giving us no incentive to shop one vendor versus another. It's only when the Rx copay plan is taken away that we notice the price differences.

> After learning this fact, one of our Smart Patient Academy students moved her longstanding prescription account from Walgreens to Costco. When she called the Walgreens pharmacist to request the transfer, the pharmacist asked why, concerned about losing her business. "Because Costco is less expensive," she said. "I checked it out online, and I can save several hundred dollars a year."
>
> The pharmacist responded by offering to give her a price match on every medicine she bought from them. She added they would match the lowest price she found anywhere locally or on the Internet. She threw in a $50 gift certificate the customer could spend on anything in the store.

Wow! That's what I call flexing our consumer muscle! Millions of small negotiations like this one will cause the cost of healthcare to decrease. Collectively, we can make the system responsive to us, but we have to be willing to flex our muscles.

Prescription Smarts before: *A bit hazy.*
Prescription Smarts after: *Clear as a bell!*

Now we'll move on to uncovering the ugly truth about primary healthcare costs…and learn to beat them in the process!

Notes & Ideas

CHAPTER 18

Pay No Attention to The Cost Behind That Curtain
The Hidden Wizardry behind Healthcare Prices

Remember the scene in The *Wizard of Oz,* where Dorothy's dog, Toto, pulls back the curtain and discovers a man pulling levers to create the illusion of a big, bad wizard?

Well, in the world of healthcare, our perception isn't much different. We've been told by insurance carriers and doctors' offices to "Pay no attention to the price behind that curtain" but, in doing so, we've been blind to rising prices. If you don't know or care what anything costs, why would you control your buying?

NEWS FLASH
I'll bet you didn't know prices can vary as much as 300%–500% between one provider and another for exactly the **same procedure**, **in the same network**, and **within the same zip code**. It's incredible, but true.

How is this possible?

Most healthcare services are priced relative to the government-set rates for Medicare.

Because the government is setting the prices, there is no relation to supply and demand. All prices outside of Medicare (meaning, in the "commercial market," where you and I live) are priced relative to Medicare.

Does this mean a Medicare patient is charged less than a non-Medicare patient?

Yes, definitely! We pay (in the "commercial market") much more than necessary to make up for the money lost in Medicare, Medicaid, and uninsured people, who don't pay their bills.

To defend yourself, you need to know the lay of the land in healthcare pricing. Let's peek behind the curtain to find out why prices vary and what to do about it!

Prices can be considered "Retail" or "Wholesale."

Part of the reason we pay premiums to insurance companies is because they're supposed to negotiate discounts off the "retail" pricing for healthcare services for our benefit. Without insurance, you would pay the "retail price"; with insurance, you pay the "wholesale price." Because you have insurance, you need to be sure you're charged the wholesale price and try to determine what that price is, before you have a procedure. You can do this by calling the billing or insurance representative in the doctor's office. In addition, wholesale prices are negotiated between insurance companies and providers, and they vary due to the negotiations. Aetna may negotiate a better wholesale price for chiropractic care than Humana, but Humana may have lower wholesale prices for cardiac care, compared to Aetna. Negotiated pricing leads to huge price variability.

Every service performed in the medical field has a digital code attached to it, not a price.
Whether in the doctor's office or an insurance company, when someone inputs one wrong digit, your routine office visit can become a leg amputation. When billing errors occur, frequently, it's a coding issue between the provider and the insurance carrier, so you want to check with the carrier first. When a doctor's office tells you they don't know what to charge you, it is because they're looking at procedure codes, not prices.

Close the curtain, quick!

This silent wizardry has worked for decades, but now there's a problem: Prices have gone up so high, some of the cost has been shifted to us. If you have a new "high-deductible health plan," you are self-insuring for your deductible, which means you, not the insurance company, pay the bill for $1,000, $2,000, or maybe $5,000 out of your pocket! And even those of us with copay plans still must reckon with high deductibles and large out-of-pocket costs when an illness strikes. With either plan, it pays to focus on the cost of care, just as we focus on the cost of any other commodity or service we buy.

"Wait, did I hear you say $5,000 a minute ago?"

Yes, you did!

How do we function in a "market," where we're not supposed to know the price of anything? We outsmart the system, that's how.

Here are a few great tips for becoming a Smart Patient for healthcare costs:

Before you go in, call and ask: *What are you going to charge me? How are you going to charge me when my plan has no copays? Can you tell me how you process the In-Network discount for me?*

Price shop at: www.fairhealthconsumer.org, www.healthcarebluebook.com, or on your insurance carrier's website (they're finally getting in the game!).

Buy a price shopping/comparison service, like Compass for $5/month for an entire family at www.compassphs.com. All of these services give you a financial and quality cost analysis, before you incur a bill, and are well worth the small, monthly fee. Ask your employer if you don't see one available.

Note: Because of the frustration in this area of healthcare, expect to see more "price transparency" services available. Your insurance carrier may also have such a service on their website.

NEWS FLASH

A Word about COBRA Prices

Remember COBRA? It's the federal law that gives you an 18-month extension of your employer benefits after you leave your job. (I know you may never quit or be laid off, but it's good to know if you might, someday, need this information.)

There is a common misconception that the price of COBRA is higher than what you were paying as an employee. In reality, it's probably only 2% higher.

Remember, while employed, you and your employer split the cost of the insurance; you likely paid only 5%–10% of the total premium.

The big shocker for you, as a new candidate for COBRA, is seeing the full premium cost. When you see that number, it will definitely make you appreciate what your employer paid on your behalf. In addition, the first bill you receive will be retroactive to the date you left employment.

That means you may see three months of premium all due at one time. Wow, that IS a big number! Just remember it's not actually a higher price.

The moral to this story?

Do your homework before you leave your job. The grass is not always greener on the other side.

You now know what's going on behind the curtain (well, as much as anyone can, anyway) and have a few ways to outsmart the system. Now let's get savvy on how to pay for those expenses with confidence, without selling your firstborn in the process!

Notes & Ideas

CHAPTER 19

How Do I Pay for All This Stuff Again?
Managing Cash Flow and Deductibles

I'll gladly pay you Thursday for an MRI today!

Whatever type of health insurance you have, it's likely you'll impact your deductible at some point and be confronted with the reality of a bill, or "shock claim," as they call it. This is the part of the health insurance world the ivory-tower types never like to talk about, because it's overwhelming and confusing to consumers.

We're going to break down the payment part into manageable bites, so you'll know how to be a Smart Patient when it comes to where your money goes.

OFFICE VISIT BILLS FOR THE HSA PLAN
If you have a High-Deductible Health Plan with no copay, the front desk person in the doctor's office may not understand what to charge you. One of three things will happen:

1. Best Option:

- You get charged nothing at the point of service.
- Provider will send the bill to the insurance company, who will apply the discount.
- Provider will send you a correct bill in the mail.

2. Next Best Option:

Provider will ask for a copay-style payment, like $30, and then send you a bill for the remainder of the balance, after they get the discount from the insurance.

3. Worst-Case Scenario:

Provider says they will collect 100% of their retail charge for the service, right now, and pay you back later. This assumes you'll take the time to hound them for your overpayment. Reimbursements can take 30–60 days, so don't pay unless you have to, and then only pay the minimum required.

Note: This is *not* a consumer-friendly approach; only accept these terms for a doctor you love and trust. Otherwise, I recommend you seek a provider who offers options #1 and/or #2.

BIG HOSPITAL BILLS FOR EVERYBODY
An "estimate" of your bill is all that's offered because:

- They don't know, beforehand, the entire scope of your medical problem and all the services they will provide.
- They also don't know what the negotiated discount, or "wholesale" price, will be once they file the claim with the insurance company.

What does the hospital do? They will ask for 100% of your deductible, up front. Sometimes, they may even make it appear that they'll withhold medical care before you pay your deductible, but hang in there and negotiate; don't be afraid to ask for what you need. And you won't be negotiating with your doctor, so you shouldn't fear a change in his treatment of you because you're being a Smart Patient. You'll be negotiating with either a Patient Advocate, Social Worker, or Case Worker, when you're in a hospital.

Here are the rules a Smart Patient should follow for the smoothest payment on medical bill totals:

RULE #1
Cash is king.

One of the biggest administrative burdens for any provider is the overhead associated with filing a claim with your insurance company. When you, as a Smart Patient, offer the provider an option of settling a bill in cash or cash equivalent (HSA card, FSA card, etc.), you're saving the business the overhead cost and time associated with the process. This cash payment option should be worth at least a 25% discount. Remember, you can file the claim with the carrier and get credit toward your deductible, so you will not have lost that credit if you're willing to do the work. Twenty-five percent of a $1,000 bill is $250. Is that worth it to you?

RULE #2
Try not to pay 100% of your deductible up front.

Don't let anyone bluff you into thinking they'll withhold care pending full payment. If they threaten such a thing, reconsider using them as a provider. This should be a big red flag.

RULE #3

You'll likely have to make a down payment for the service.

Try for $0, but be prepared to offer 25% of your deductible, then work out payments. Providers negotiate about 60–70% of the time, but not always. You won't know if you don't ask.

RULE #4

When paying off multiple medical providers, pay the fastest bill-er to your insurance company first.

The insurance company whittles down your total deductible, based on who files claims *fastest*. **Note**: The fastest biller may not be the source of the biggest bill.

RULE #5

Try to push the largest billers to file the claim with your insurer faster—usually the hospital.

This will speed the process of satisfying your deductible expense, so insurance will pay 100% soon.

RULE #6

Use pre-tax dollars to pay for these bills.

This will save you about 20% right off the top, using an HSA card or a Flexible Spending Account (FSA) card. Remember, you can use these dollars to pay for anything medically necessary for any legal dependent in your family, whether or not they're covered on your health plan!

RULE #7

In cases of non-emergency, use providers who are "friendly billers," not those who threaten to withhold care or drag their feet on billing your insurer.

A friendly biller will work with you on payment plans, negotiated discounts, and timely filing to your insurance company, so you get credit for meeting your deductible.

This is the essence of "consumer driven health care"—the consumer votes with their dollars and repeat business. When patients demand to be treated like customers, they will be treated as such. Until that time, the roles are reversed, and healthcare will continue to be about the providers, not the patient.

Remember: Except for emergency and urgent care situations, you can choose your providers.

You and I, as consumers, have some control, if we're willing to use it.

Ask and You Shall Receive

If there's one rule to remember about being a Smart Patient, it's this: Doctors and hospitals will negotiate large medical bills that make up your deductible and arrange payment plans, but only if you ask. There's no sign telling you this, so you need to be aware as you enter any medical setting, where you will be paying a large chunk of your deductible.

Here's how this works in practice: You may recall me mentioning I had surgery, recently, to treat a tumor near my brain stem. We had a deductible on our health plan of $3,000. (You should know, by now, any surgery will hit your deductible on any plan you have, right?)

On the day of the surgery, we asked: "Can we give you a $500 down payment and pay you $250 for the next ten months?" (I say "we," but it was my wife, Cary, who did this negotiation, as I was too nervous to care—working as a team is critical.) They agreed, so we pulled out our trusty HSA debit card and paid them $500 pre-tax dollars. (The payment plan bought us the time we needed to find the rest of the money to fund our HSA account.) After making three months of payments, we owed them a balance of $1,750. We asked: "Would you take $1,250, today, if I could pay the balance right now?" Again, they agreed. The result? A $500 savings and a much more comfortable cash-flow management situation that fit our budget constraints.

Bonus: Because I could time this surgery, we scheduled it in January, so we would meet our deductible at the beginning of the calendar year. That gave us the rest of the year with 100% coverage on our health plan. That was eleven more months with no additional out-of-pocket medical expenses.

Cool, eh?

Although utilizing doctors and health insurance and the ensuing cost of doing so is necessary for most of us, there are ways we can curb those costs and visits by focusing on our wellness.

Notes & Ideas

CHAPTER 20

What? No More Cheetos?
How Companies Are Motivating Good Lifestyle Choices

Aren't I in good enough shape already?

If you've seen the show *Mad Men,* about the advertising firm on Madison Avenue in the 1960s, you know Don Draper, our advertising hero, smokes and drinks his way through the day, as does everybody on the show. You may be shocked by this or think, "Those were the days!" (I admit, it makes me want a martini, right now!)

Fast forward to the *Mad Men*-style show of the future that looks back on *our* corporate life, today. When viewers see super-sized fast food lunches on the run, bowls of candy in nearly every office, and breakrooms chock-full of birthday cake and junk food, people will shake their heads and say, "Wow, how did we live like that?"

If you've not yet noticed, the era of "Corporate Wellness" has arrived and, like it or not, your participation is being politely requested. For engaging in these programs, you're rewarded with incentives, like gift certificates or even cash, proverbial "carrots" to motivate you toward better lifestyle choices that equate to better health. What's the cost of *not* participating?

Why is this intrusion into our personal lives coming on so strong? Because, according to the Centers for Disease Control:

> The majority of America's staggering $2.6 trillion healthcare tab (as of 2010) was spent treating lifestyle diseases. While we worry about healthcare costs rising 8% or 9% a year, we spend over 50% of our costs on diseases, caused mostly by the way we choose to behave.

Since we're all feeling the pinch of healthcare expenses, doesn't it make sense to do something about it? Think of it this way: You, your co-workers, and all of your dependents are in the same healthcare claims boat, together. Our rates go up or down, depending on how healthy we are as a group. This is how your health status can affect the pocketbook of your co-worker.

Knowing that, is this sudden interest in wellness making sense?

I hate to say it, but changing engrained habits, especially bad ones, and the way people live is a slow process. Naturally, healthy people are receptive, because they're already on the wellness bandwagon. But the couch potatoes? Well, they respond only to financial pain.

What types of penalties can we expect?

You're already seeing higher premiums for smokers and fines for not taking a Health Risk Assessment (those forms where they ask you all those lifestyle questions) or participating in organized Wellness Programs at work.

My advice to you: Take advantage of the Wellness Program your company offers. Use the *Fitbit* they bought for you. You can fight it or join it. I suggest you join it. You'll save money, time and, maybe, your life.

Notes & Ideas

CHAPTER 21

The $10,000 Ski Lift Ticket
Why Accident Plans Can Be a Great Investment

Remember when we reviewed what kind of healthcare consumer you were? Well, I don't know about you, but my family and I are in the *Disaster Man/Woman* category. This example involves my wife, Cary.

In March 2012, we went skiing in Santa Fe, New Mexico. All was well until…yep, you guessed it…an accident occurred. Cary is the proud owner of a metal plate and seven screws in her right knee, and I'm the proud payer of a $10,000 deductible on a $28,000 hospital bill. OUCH!

"But wait," you may say, "aren't you insurance guys supposed to know how to cut risk?" Yes, we are, and you can do it, too, by taking two steps:

1. Get a family accident plan (widely offered voluntarily through your work), especially if you have an HSA plan or a high-deductible copay plan.

2. Negotiate your bills with the providers. Here's how this worked in our case:

$10,000 deductible

–$5,000 covered by the accident plan (50% of my de-ductible for the entire family)

–$2,600 negotiated—by us—off the remainder of the bill with the surgeon and physical therapists

=$2,400 total out-of-pocket expense on a $10,000 charge

Not bad, eh?

And here's how this summed up for us in a great way:

Since our $10,000 deductible was met with only $2,400 out-of-pocket on our end, my plan now covers 100% of all medical bills for my family for the remainder of the calendar year. (Wow! Perhaps, it's time to get that hair transplant I've been waiting for!)

Bottom line: The process isn't difficult, and the plan's available to most everyone. I've personally never lost money buying an accident plan for my entire family—it's well worth it, when you have health insurance with high deductibles and high out-of-pocket potential. The cost of a typical plan should be about

$15/month for one person and about $40/month for a family of five.

My advice? Try it.

Notes & Ideas

CONCLUSION

Congratulations! You have read a book about health insurance and patient care, and you lived to talk about it! You should feel like you have the world in your hand.

You are equipped to save hundreds, maybe even thousands, of dollars. That's something to crow about!

Here's to your best health!

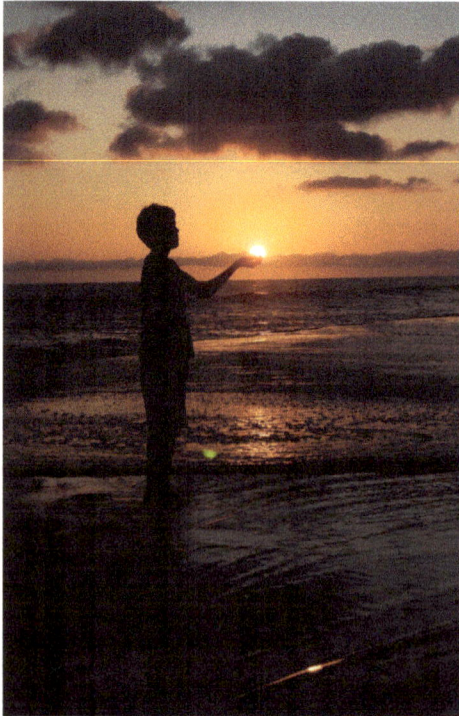

Helpful Resources

Smart Patient Academy's *The Opportunity Coach*
Download the application for emotional fitness:
www.smartpatientacademy.com

Functional Medicine
To find a functional medicine provider:
www.functionalmedicine.org

Quality Integrative Medicine:
To find high quality integrative providers:
www.AIHM.org

Personal Health Journals
To keep family and friends informed:
www.caringbridge.org

Hospital Safety Scores
To find out the hospital safety scores in your area:
www.hospitalsafetyscores.com

Adaptive Movement
High Performance with disabilities:
www.iamadaptive.com

Patient Communities
Find other patients like you and learn:
www.smartpatients.com
www.patientslikeme.com
www.participatorymedicine.org

Credible Medical Info
To learn about medical conditions:
www.healthline.com
www.webmd.com

Expert Second Opinion Services
To confirm a diagnosis or find the best care protocols:
www.bestdoctors.com

Patient Navigation
To hire, learn what a navigator can do for you:
www.patientnavigator.com

Patient Advocacy
To hire, learn what a patient advocate can do for you:
www.npaf.org

Mindfulness Resources
State of the art meditation techniques:
www.mindvalley.com

HSA Related
To set up or log into an HSA account:
www.hsabank.com

Rx Shopping Related

To compare prescription drug costs by location and to find generics:

www.goodrx.com

Medical Procedures Pricing Related

To determine costs of medical and dental care by CPT code:

www.healthcarebluebook.com

Price Shopping Services

To purchase a concierge price shopping service:

www.compassphs.com

Your Explanation of Benefits and In-Network MDs

www.[YourInsuranceCarrier'sWebsite].com

ABOUT THE AUTHOR

Jim Skinner is an entrepreneur, author, avid sportsman, and family man, who lives and works in the Central Texas Hill Country. A native of Southern California, he grew up surfing and traveling in Costa Rica and Spain. His education is wide and varied, including a Bachelor of Arts Degree in Spanish Literature from the University of California San Diego and a Master's Degree in Latin American Studies from Georgetown University. His fluency in Spanish and his unique background enabled him to work in national security in Washington, DC and as a White House political appointee as the Executive Director to the President's Advisory Board for Cuba Broadcasting.

In 1994, he moved his family to Texas, where he started a new career in the health and life insurance brokerage field. When asked, "Why Texas?" Jim says: "Texas provided a family-oriented, high-quality life, low cost of living, and proximity to Mexico and Latin America. The location was also a good halfway point between family in Florida and California."

After working several years in the insurance field, Jim was diagnosed, at age 42, with a genetic form of colon cancer that had progressed to stage three by the time it was discovered. He underwent twelve months of chemo, a lifetime dose of radiation, and colon surgery. Four years later, he underwent Gamma Knife surgery to treat an unrelated tumor near his brain stem. That surgery left him with no balance and deaf on his left side. These and numerous other less serious medical situations have given Jim deep-dive experiences into the medical field, which influence all of his writing and training in the insurance field.

Jim is the founder and president of the Smart Patient Academy, an insurance benefits enrollment and communications company, based in Texas. Jim is also host of an iTunes podcast, called Stories with A Purpose, which is collection of incredible stories of people successfully navigating through major medical challenges. His sister company, JMS Benefit Solutions, is an insurance brokerage and consulting firm that works with mid-size employer groups, both domestic and foreign owned. He does life insurance planning for executives, through which he has developed a unique expertise in helping clientele from Mexico.

Jim continues to be an avid surfer, rock climber, and skateboarder. In 2009, he and his family celebrated the grand opening of JAWS Skatepark in New Braunfels, Texas. With support from the Tony Hawk Foundation, his family raised over $500,000 to create a state-of-the-art, public skateboard park, which is enjoyed by about 150,000 skaters each year. Jim and his boys can be found there most weekends.

Jim and his wife, Cary, have been married 30+ years and have three children: Michelle, Jamie, and Will.

JAWS Skatepark grand opening with the Skinner Skaters, June 2009.

www.ingramcontent.com/pod-product-compliance
Lightning Source LLC
Chambersburg PA
CBHW072137020426
42334CB00018B/1840